Political Campaigns

Open for Debate

Political Campaigns

Corinne J. Naden

Marshall Cavendish
Benchmark
New York

With thanks to Kevin Arceneaux, Ph.D., assistant professor, Department of Political Science and Institute for Public Affairs, faculty affiliate, Temple University, Philadelphia.

Marshall Cavendish Benchmark
99 White Plains Road
Tarrytown, NY 10591-5502
www.marshallcavendish.us

Library of Congress Cataloging-in-Publication Data
Naden, Corinne J.
Political campaigns / by Corinne J. Naden.
p. cm. — (Open for debate)
Includes bibliographical references and index.
ISBN 978-0-7614-2944-9
1. Political campaigns. 2. Elections. I. Title. II. Series.

JF1001.N19 2008
324.7—dc22

2007022594

Photo research by Lindsay Aveilhe/Linda Sykes
Picture Research, Inc., Hilton Head, SC

Images.com/Corbis: cover, 6; Lisa Hornak/Reuters: 8 top; Tami Chappell/
Reuters: 8 bottom; The Granger Collection: 11, 27, 53; Nicholas Kamm/AFP/Getty Images;
23; Mark Wilson/Getty Images: 29; Time and Life Pictures/Getty Images: 33; Joseph Sohm/
Visions of America/Corbis RF: 38; Bettmann/Corbis: 40, 77, 91, 94; AP Photo/Gush-
Cheney 2004: 47 bottom; AP Photo: 47 top; Monika Graff/The Image Works: 63; Corbis:
66; Steve Goldstein/Corbis: 69; David J. & Janice L. Frent Collection/Corbis: 84; Shawn
Thew/epa/Corbis: 86; Robert King/Getty Images: 99; Tim Graham/Corbis: 105;
Sergio Dorantes/Sygma/Corbis: 111; AFP/Getty Images: 115.

Publisher: Michelle Bisson
Art Director: Anahid Hamparian
Series Designer: Sonia Chaghatzbanian

Printed in Malaysia

1 3 5 6 4 2

Contents

Introduction

Every four years in November, the United States chooses a president to lead the country. The winner is elected by a plurality of popular votes and a majority of votes in the electoral college. But whoever becomes president in any given year is, in one sense, always elected long before November. The U.S. election process is the now customary, often peculiar, and always drawn-out event known as the presidential campaign. Some people are perplexed by its methods. Some are annoyed by its methods. Some wonder how it accomplishes anything at all.

There is little open debate about whether political campaigns should exist in the United States. There is, however, much debate over almost everything else about them. Perhaps that should not be surprising. For good or bad the U.S. electoral process is unique. Many democracies throughout the world elect their leaders. But no one does it exactly like Americans do. The process in the United States is confusing, lengthy, expensive, sometimes dividing, and sometimes uniting. It is constantly changing, constantly evolving. Everyone seems to have an opinion on what should be changed, from the time a candidate first says "I'm running" until the last voting machine is closed on election day.

THE DEMOCRATIC PROCESS IS A LENGTHY ONE. (ABOVE) THE ORIGINAL CANDIDATES FOR THE REPUBLICAN PRESIDENTIAL NOMINATION POSE BEFORE THEIR NEW HAMPSHIRE DEBATE. FROM LEFT TO RIGHT: TOM TANCREDO, RON PAUL, MIKE HUCKABEE, RUDY GIULIANI, MITT ROMNEY, JOHN MCCAIN, AND SAM BROWNBACK.

(BELOW) THE ORIGINAL DEMOCRATIC PRESIDENTIAL NOMINEES POSE BEFORE THEIR DEBATE IN SOUTH CAROLINA ON JULY 23, 2007. FROM LEFT TO RIGHT: CHRIS DODD, JOHN EDWARDS, HILLARY CLINTON, BARACK OBAMA, BILL RICHARDSON, JOE BIDEN, AND DENNIS KUCINICH.

Political Campaigns takes a close look at this peculiarly American process. It discusses the major issues that are still challenged and remain open for debate: campaign funding; why incumbents have a better shot at winning; how so-called soft money helps the Republicans win; and the importance of primaries. For the November 2008 campaign, state primaries (the earliest vote counts) began in January. How much do these early primaries determine the vote in November? What is the emerging importance of electronic voting? When George W. Bush ran against Al Gore in 2000, the election hinged on a dispute over voting machines. How does dirty campaigning affect the final vote? What is the effect of voter fraud and other illegalities at the polls? How is campaigning on the Internet changing the voting process?

At each presidential election, there are calls for changes in the way Americans elect their leaders. Can the process be made simpler, more fair, less expensive, shorter, and less complicated? Some people have suggested making the entire nominating process depend on a one-day national primary. Another idea calls for primaries in four geographic regions. At their convention for the 2000 campaign, Republicans rejected the proposed Delaware Plan, which divided the states into four groups according to population. Backers of these plans say they would eliminate the push for earlier and earlier state primaries to get the edge on voter interest. But many disagree, and the debate goes on.

After each presidential election, political campaigning slips into the background for most Americans. But not for all. The peculiar institution is already looking ahead to the next election. Americans have been electing presidents since George Washington took office in 1789. The debate is not about whether the process works. It is and continues to be about whether we can make it work better.

1
Party Time

People fiercely debate every aspect of U.S. political campaigns, but most seem to agree on one thing: They go on too long. Voters have hardly learned the names of the latest winners before some of the new hopefuls hit the next campaign trail. The Founding Fathers would not recognize this kind of campaign. Not only were there no political campaigns when the nation began, but there were no political parties to campaign for. In fact, the Founding Fathers were against the idea of political parties, which James Madison referred to as "factions." In *The Federalist No. 10*, he wrote, "By a faction, I understand a number of citizens, whether amounting to a majority or a minority of the whole, who are united and actuated by some common impulse of passion, or of interest, adversed to the rights of other citizens or to the permanent and aggregate interests of the community."

The Founding Fathers were against political parties because they believed national leaders should be above local or sectional prejudices and interests. George Washington

THIS 1793 CARTOON RIDICULES THE ANTI-FEDERALIST PARTY AS AN UNRULY MOB OPPOSED TO GOVERNMENT AND IN LEAGUE WITH THE DEVIL. JEFFERSON IS SHOWN STANDING ON THE TABLE, MAKING A SPEECH.

felt that laws should be passed strictly for the good of the nation, not because of personal views. Indeed, when he became president, he tried to keep his personal feelings out of politics. This sometimes made him seem detached and aloof to his colleagues. Such calmness annoyed Vice President John Adams to the point that he referred to the president as "an old mutton head." However, before the end of Washington's second term, the personal views of the nation's leaders were already dividing into what became political parties.

In 1789 and in 1792, for the only times in U.S. history, the president was elected without any opposition. (In the election of 1820, no one ran against James Monroe. However, elector William Plumer of New Hampshire wrote in the name of John Quincy Adams on his ballot. He said he wanted George Washington to be the only president who was elected unanimously.) The members of the Electoral College, who were named to choose a president, never considered anyone but Washington. In fact probably the only person who doubted that he should take the office was Washington himself. He was uneasy about accepting the job. This was partly because when he retired from the army, he said his retirement was going to be permanent. But Washington was a war hero and a man everyone admired. So he accepted the presidency with resolve and dignity. And that was the way he ran the office.

The Electoral System

The Constitutional Convention met in 1787 to write a constitution for the brand new nation. One of the concerns was how to elect a president. Three suggestions were offered: Let Congress do it, let the state legislatures do it, or let the people vote directly. All three were rejected. Instead it was decided that a U.S. president would be elected through the Electoral College. The idea was to have the most knowledgeable and informed people from each state cast their votes for the leader. The system was intended to work without political parties or political campaigns.

Each state had the same number of electors as its two senators plus its number of U.S. representatives. (The number of representatives is based on state population.) Each elector cast two votes for president. The candidate who received the most votes became president. The candidate with the next most votes became vice president. Since no one thought of political parties at the time, no one thought that the president and vice president might hold different political views. Section I, Article II in the Constitution mentions the possibility of a tie vote in the Electoral College, which is what happened in the presidential election of 1800. (The Electoral College requires a majority, not a plurality, vote for the winner. Majority means a number greater than half of the total; plurality means having more votes than the other candidate or candidates, whatever the total.) Thomas Jefferson and Aaron Burr got an equal number of electoral votes. The House of Representatives broke the tie with a vote for Jefferson.

But no one wanted that to happen again. The Twelfth Amendment to the Constitution, ratified in 1804, requires each elector to cast one vote for president and one for vice president. In case no presidential candidate gets a majority of electoral votes, the House of Representatives casts the deciding vote.

The Electoral College is still a source of debate among Americans. All states except Maine and Nebraska have a winner-take-all popular vote for electors. That means that the candidate with the most popular votes in the state gets all the state's electoral votes. With this system it is possible for the new president to lose the popular vote. That is what happened in the 2000 election when Al Gore won the popular vote by 537,149, but George W. Bush received the most electoral votes.

Those who oppose this system say that the election of 2000 (and also the elections of 1876 between Rutherford B. Hayes and Samuel Tilden and 1888 between Benjamin Harrison and Grover Cleveland) undermined the presidency. They feel that the winner-take-all approach encourages a candidate to concentrate on the larger states and ignore smaller ones. A candidate could win the election by winning just eleven states. Taking the ten largest states plus either Virginia or Georgia would mean winning 270 electoral votes, and that's enough to win the election.

Those who back the winner-take-all system disagree. They point out that a candidate would rarely adopt a strategy of concentrating on the ten largest states simply because he or she could not be sure of winning them. In addition all states get two electors for senators regardless of population. Therefore the smaller states get more weight in the Electoral College with this system than if it were based purely on the popular vote.

Agree to Disagree

In 1792 Washington was elected for a second term, although he did not campaign for it. According to *Hats in the Ring*, "Washington devised no electoral strategies, made no campaign trips, did no fund-raising, delivered no stirring campaign speeches, attended no political conventions." It would not be long before all that would change.

By the end of his first term even the even-tempered Washington could not keep others from disagreeing over such matters as foreign debt and the proper range of central government power. The feud that had begun during the debates over the Constitution continued to grow. From those early debates came the beginning of two differing political camps. It was also the beginning of political parties in the United States.

The main opposing leaders in Washington's administration were Secretary of the Treasury Alexander Hamilton and Secretary of State Thomas Jefferson. Hamilton's economic policies favored the more industrial north. Jefferson backed the agrarian, slaveholding southern states. At one point Washington was so disgusted with their feuding that he refused to serve a second term. Hamilton and Jefferson and their followers united long enough to change his mind, however.

Washington left office in 1797. By that time the loose alliances that had formed around Hamilton and Jefferson

How the Electoral College Works

It may sound surprising, but the people of Russia have a more direct presidential election process than Americans do. The person who wins the majority of votes in Russia wins the election. But Americans do not directly elect their presidents and vice presidents. Instead they choose *electors*, who make up the Electoral College. The electors cast the votes for the nation's two top jobs.

Who chooses the electors? The political parties in each state submit a list of people who are pledged to their candidate for president. The list goes to the state's chief election official. Members of Congress or those who work for the federal government cannot be named as electors. The number of electors in each state is equal to the number of senators (two for each state) plus the number of U.S. representatives (based on population). For instance Nebraska is a state with a small population, so it has three U.S. representatives plus two senators, for a total of five electors. New York has a large population; it has thirty-one U.S. representatives, plus two senators, for a total of thirty-three electors.

Candidates for the Senate and the House of Representatives are generally chosen in primary elections that are usually held several months before the general elections. Members of the Senate, the smaller body that has 100 members, serve six-year terms. The House of Representatives has 435 members who are elected for two-year terms.

had unofficial names. They were the nation's first political parties. Hamilton and his supporters, who included Washington and Vice President John Adams, were called Federalists. (Washington never actually joined the party, but he supported its principles.) They acknowledged the ultimate power of the people, but they also believed in rule by a well-educated elite. That idea appealed to landowners, bankers, and industrialists. As John Jay, first chief justice of the Supreme Court, was fond of saying, "The people who own the country ought to govern it." Federalists believed in a loose interpretation of the Constitution and paid little attention to states' rights. Jefferson called them monarchists, but they vehemently denied the accusation.

Jefferson's backers were called Anti-Federalists or Democratic-Republicans. They had more trust in the people and placed less emphasis on a ruling elite group. They felt that a strong federal government would take power away from the people and would not be likely to respect their rights. They favored states' rights and favored farmers over bankers and industrialists. This party was known by various names, such as Jeffersonians or Republicans (no relation to the modern Republican Party). It was the dominant political party in the United States from 1800 until 1820. Three of its members became president: Jefferson in 1800 and 1804, James Madison in 1808 and 1812, and James Monroe in 1816 and 1820. By 1824 the party split into various factions. By the mid–1830s, the Democratic-Republicans referred to themselves as Democrats. The name was not officially changed until 1844.

Another party that gained attention in the first half of the nineteenth century was the Whig Party, founded by Senator Henry Clay and other fiscal conservatives. The name came from a political group in England and signified rebellion. It was formed in the United States to oppose Andrew Jackson and the Democratic Party, and it was active from 1832 to 1856. For a time it was the second major political party in the United States. Whigs elected two presidents: William Henry Harrison in 1840 and Zachary Taylor in 1848. Both died in office. By mid-century the country was so polarized over slavery that the Whig party died. Most Northern Whigs joined the newly formed Republican Party, while most Southern Whigs became Democrats, advocating states' rights.

The Major Political Parties

In 1942 political scientist E. E. Schattschneider remarked that "modern democracy is unthinkable save in terms of parties." Since the nation was founded, all but eight people who served as president of the United States have belonged to either the Republican or Democratic Party, the two major U.S. political parties. Although third-party candidates have often run for president, either a Democrat or Republican has been elected since 1852.

Even though it is called the GOP—for Grand Old Party—the Republicans are the younger of the two major groups. Since Richard Nixon was elected in 1968, Republican presidents have won the White House eight times, although not consecutively. Republicans held the majority in the U.S. Senate almost continuously from 1995 to 2007, and they were the majority party in the House from 1994 to when this title went to press in 2007.

The Republicans became a national party in 1856 when John C. Frémont was nominated with the slogan "Free soil, Free labor, Free speech, Free men, Frémont." The Republicans were considered a third party at the time, with the Democrats and Whigs the two major parties. Yet Frémont took 33 percent of the vote. Four years later Abraham Lincoln became the nation's first Republican president.

Presidents and Their Parties

George Washington	1789, 1792	
John Adams	1796	Federalist
Thomas Jefferson	1800, 1804	Democratic-Republican
James Madison	1808, 1812	Democratic-Republican
James Monroe	1816, 1820	Democratic-Republican
John Quincy Adams	1824	Democratic-Republican
Andrew Jackson	1828, 1832	Democratic
Martin Van Buren	1836	Democratic
William H. Harrison	1840	Whig
John Tyler	1841	Whig
James K. Polk	1844	Democratic
Zachary Taylor	1848	Whig
Millard Fillmore	1850	Whig
Franklin Pierce	1852	Democratic
James Buchanan	1856	Democratic
Abraham Lincoln	1860, 1864	Republican (temporary name change in 1864 to National Union or Union Republican Party)

Andrew Johnson	1865	Republican
Ulysses S. Grant	1868, 1872	Republican
Rutherford B. Hayes	1876	Republican
James Garfield	1880	Republican
Chester A. Arthur	1881	Republican
Grover Cleveland	1884, 1892	Democratic
Benjamin Harrison	1888	Republican
William McKinley	1896, 1900	Republican
Theodore Roosevelt	1901, 1904	Republican
William Howard Taft	1908	Republican
Woodrow Wilson	1912, 1916	Democratic
Warren G. Harding	1920	Republican
Calvin Coolidge	1923, 1924	Republican
Herbert Hoover	1928	Republican
Franklin D. Roosevelt	1932, 1936, 1940, 1944	Democratic
Harry S. Truman	1945, 1948	Democratic
Dwight D. Eisenhower	1952, 1956	Republican
John F. Kennedy	1960	Democratic
Lyndon B. Johnson	1963, 1964	Democratic
Richard M. Nixon	1968, 1972	Republican
Gerald R. Ford	1974	Republican
James E. Carter	1976	Democratic
Ronald Reagan	1980, 1984	Republican
George H. W. Bush	1988	Republican
William J. Clinton	1992, 1996	Democratic
George W. Bush	2000, 2004	Republican

The Republican Party is generally the more socially conservative of the two major parties. It traditionally has closer ties to large corporations and locally owned businesses. It gets little support from labor unions. Republicans favor limited government interference on economic issues. In fact, in his first inaugural address on January 20, 1981, Republican President Ronald Reagan said, "government is not the solution to our problem; government is the problem." However, Republicans do support intervention on social issues such as abortion. In general most Republicans favor capital punishment, the rights of gun owners, and welfare benefit reductions. They oppose abortion, same-sex marriage, and racial quotas. The party's religious wing tends to support organized prayer in public schools.

The nation's other major political group, the Democrats, is the oldest continuing political party in the world. It traces its origins to the Democratic-Republican Party founded by Jefferson in 1792. In 1828 Andrew Jackson became the first president to be elected on the Democratic ticket. Much of the party's current philosophy stems from 1932 and Franklin D. Roosevelt's pro–working class ideas. However, the Democrats suffered a string of lost elections in the White House and the Congress during the late 1900s. After that many Democrats favored a shift from the liberal left to more centrist policies.

Democrats usually back farmers, workers, and labor unions. In general they support civil liberties, equal rights, welfare programs, and abortion rights. The party tends to believe that government should play a role in reducing poverty and social injustice, even if that means more government intervention and higher taxes. Many Democrats favor a national health-care system. Since the 1970s environmental issues have also been a high priority on the Democratic agenda.

In 1992, for the first time in twelve years, a Democrat was elected to the White House. William Jefferson (Bill)

Clinton of Hope, Arkansas, defeated the incumbent, George Herbert Walker Bush. A major issue was a serious economic recession. In fact, during the campaign, Clinton kept a three-word message at his campaign headquarters. It said simply: "The economy, stupid." Clinton won handily, 370 electoral votes to 168, with third-party candidate Ross Perot taking no electoral votes.

The Role of Third Parties

The United States historically has a two-party system. Why are there only two viable parties? In the United States politics have been nationalized. The two major parties can compete across local districts. In other countries—India, for example—local politics can and sometimes do overshadow national politics so that viable third parties emerge.

Third parties in the United States have long participated in national and state elections with varying degrees of success. Though they have never won a national election, their candidates play an important role in a democratic government. Third parties are often organized around one major issue, which often attracts voters to the polls. Such issues may be ignored—at least initially—by the major parties. Ralph Nader's concern with clean air and auto safety standards in the 2000 election is an example. Sometimes an issue brought up by a third-party candidate finds its way into a major party platform.

One of the reasons that third parties have had limited success is that they often have difficulty just getting on the ballot. Laws that give access to voting ballots vary throughout the states. They are often very restrictive. With tight resources, a third-party candidate may not have the means to get his or her name on the ballot. Some states require a third party to obtain thousands of signatures from registered voters just to list the party's candidates on the ballot. One third-party candidate who did win national recognition for a time was Jesse Ventura of the Reform Party (later the Minnesota Independence Party). A former professional wrestler, navy veteran, and actor, he was governor of Minnesota from 1999 to 2003.

A popular election philosophy says that a vote for a third-party candidate is wasted. It won't elect the third party, but it takes away from a possible major-party winner. In modern times no third-party candidate has been elected president, but some have made a difference in the outcomes. At the very least they gave the major contenders a good scare.

The 1860 election, for instance, had four major candidates: John C. Breckenridge for the Southern Democrats, John Bell for the Constitutional Union Party, Stephen A. Douglas for the Northern Democrats, and Abraham Lincoln on the Republican ticket. Lincoln won with only 39 percent of the popular vote, and he was not even on the ballot in many states.

In 1912 Theodore Roosevelt ran on the Bull Moose ticket and got 88 electoral votes out of a possible 531. He lost to Democrat Woodrow Wilson.

Strom Thurmond ran as an anti-integration Dixiecrat in 1948, and Henry Wallace headed the Progressive Party ticket. Despite the split in the Democratic vote, Harry Truman upset Republican Thomas E. Dewey.

In 1992 Ross Perot and his Reform Party aided the success of Bill Clinton over George H. W. Bush. Ralph Nader ran on the Green Party ticket in 2000 and is often credited (or blamed) with helping George W. Bush in a controversial victory over Al Gore.

David Cobb headed the Green Party in the 2004 election. He and Michael Badnarik of the Libertarian Party were arrested for trying to cross police lines to get into the televised presidential debate between the two major candidates, George W. Bush and John Kerry.

THE NEWS THAT THE DEMOCRATS HAD RETAKEN THE HOUSE OF REPRESEN-TATIVES IN NOVEMBER 2006 WAS BIG NEWS—NEWSPAPERS ACROSS THE COUNTRY BLARED IT IN IDENTICAL HEADLINES.

The 2006 midterm elections were a smashing victory for the Democrats, who took control of both houses of Congress. The voters were in revolt mainly against President Bush's handling of the war in Iraq. Pollsters say that a number of incumbents lost their seats to the Democrats because third-party candidates split the vote.

2
Who's in Charge?

Once political parties developed in the United States, there had to be some way to let the voters know what they stood for. What does it mean if candidate X says he's a Democrat? Do you want to vote for candidate Y if she's running on the Green Party ticket?

Before political parties were in full swing, U.S. election campaigns were relatively sedate and proper affairs. But that changed after 1840. According to Richard McCormick in his study of American presidential politics, "The presidential game had now become a kind of mass folk festival [with] the enthusiasms of religious revivalism and the passions of a bloodless internal war."

This mass folk festival is known as the political campaign. A very old tactic, it is the way in which most candidates get their messages to the voting public. A campaign is an organized effort to influence decisions made by a group. Political campaigns on national, state, and local levels try to persuade qualified American voters to choose a particular person and party. But political campaigns exist on many levels. Choosing a senior class president, for instance, is a political campaign. There are campaigns against smoking. In 1985 Tipper Gore, the former vice president's wife, headed a campaign against suggestive lyrics in rock music.

In the United States, elections—and election campaigns —occur frequently. There are different types of elections and different political offices to run for, from national president to local sheriff, from head of the school board to head of a political union. Except for judicial elections in some states, all state and national elections in the United States are partisan. Candidates from different political parties are pitted against each other.

Modern Campaign Elements

To be successful any modern political campaign has to be effective in at least three ways:

(1) It must get its message across. For example, this candidate will cut your taxes, and that's why you should vote for her!

(2) It must be good at raising money. Especially today, when so much campaigning consists of expensive television ads, fund-raising is crucial.

(3) It needs great staff members. These are the key players on the presidential campaign team:

Campaign manager, in charge of the entire operation;

Chief fund-raiser, in charge of raising money according to the finance laws;

Press secretary, in charge of relations with the news media;

Pollster, in charge of conducting polls that keep track of support for the candidate in certain areas;

Media consultant, in charge of advertising.

Other essential workers include the staff members and the so-called foot soldiers. These are the party believers and activists who do all the drudge work. They make the endless phone calls to party members to remind them to vote. In addition to this base, they are interested in talking to swing voters who might listen to their message, as opposed to trying to reach those who are loyal to the opposing side. They canvass door-to-door to explain party issues or to detail a candidate's stand on a particular issue. When all of these tasks are performed well and voters believe the message, the end result may be an election victory.

Another important tool for the modern election campaign is the use of political consultants. These professional people advise and assist in political campaigns. Each party employs professionals who use highly sophisticated management tools to convey the party's message. Consultants primarily are involved in the party's use of paid media, mainly television. However, they are also involved in just about all aspects of political campaigning. One of the first known political consultants was Mark Hanna, political advisor to William McKinley (1897–1901). The first established consulting firm was Campaigns, Inc., which started in California in the 1930s.

Besides their work for the politician or party, consultants increasingly find themselves the center of attention. They are often sought after for their political views. An example is James Carville, political consultant to Bill Clinton in the 1990s, who still appears on many TV news programs.

According to the authors of *Political Parties, Interest Groups, and Political Campaigns:* "In some ways, the contemporary Republican and Democratic parties resemble midsized corporations," with permanent headquarters, top executives, and many employees. Actually, the authors point out, "each major party is a complex network of

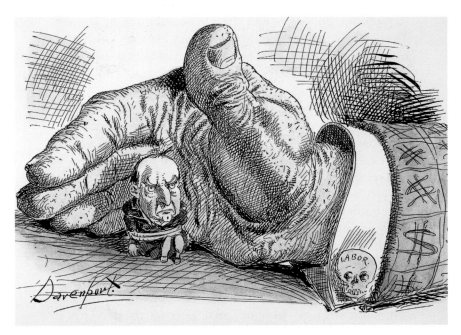

MARK HANNA WAS THE FIRST PAID POLITICAL CONSULTANT, BUT WILLIAM MCKINLEY WAS FAR FROM THE LAST PRESIDENT PORTRAYED AS BEING PUTTY IN THE HANDS OF HIS MANAGERS. THIS CARTOON SHOWING MCKINLEY IN THE PALM OF HANNA'S HAND APPEARED IN THE *NEW YORK JOURNAL* DURING THE MID-1890S.

organizations with overlapping responsibilities and decentralized power."

Both parties have national committees that are headquartered in Washington, D.C. The committees promote the goals of the party. The main goals are, of course, to occupy the White House and to elect as many congressional members as possible.

The Republican National Committee (RNC) is responsible for campaign strategy and tactics during presidential and other campaigns. It advertises the goals of the president when the GOP is in the White House. It explains

Republican policies when the Democrats are in control. The RNC is headed by a chairperson (usually, but not always, a man), who is chosen by a sitting U.S. president. If there is no sitting U.S. president, the state committees choose the chairperson.

During a presidential election campaign the RNC decides on campaign strategy. It raises money for Republican candidates and supervises the national convention. Republican committees in the House and Senate raise millions of dollars for each election cycle. All RNC activities are approved by the sitting president or candidate. Throughout the country, state and large city committees operate for the party in much the same way. However, the RNC has by far the most money and influence on campaign strategy and tactics.

The Democratic National Committee (DNC) works in much the same way as the RNC. It is mostly focused on campaign strategy. In a national election the DNC is in charge of the convention. In all the campaigning that leads to an election, the DNC raises funds and coordinates strategy. If the Democrats are in the White House, the chairperson of the DNC is usually chosen by the president. Otherwise the DNC members select the chairperson. After the Democrats lost the national election in 2004, members elected Howard Dean, former governor of Vermont, for a four-year term as DNC president. He had campaigned for the Democratic presidential nomination that year but lost it to John Kerry, who then lost the election to George W. Bush.

Party Platforms

All political parties have a platform. The major parties adopt a new platform every four years at their national convention. The platform is a list of principles and beliefs

HOWARD DEAN LOST HIS CHANCE FOR THE DEMOCRATIC NOMINATION TO THE PRESIDENCY EARLY IN THE 2004 RACE, BUT HE BECAME HEAD OF THE DEMOCRATIC NATIONAL COMMITTEE AFTER THE ELECTION.

that the party supports. It tells voters what party members intend to do if they are elected to office. If the platform appeals to the general public, the party's candidates will probably be elected. The platform is usually a list of the party's support for or opposition to a topic, such as stem cell research or same-sex marriage. Each topic is called a plank.

Both major parties elect a committee of 186 members who draft the platform. Any party member is eligible to serve on the committee, and all members may contribute suggestions. The party votes to adopt the platform during the Republican or Democratic convention, a few months before the November election. At each convention the candidates are formally chosen to run.

By the time of the convention, adopting the party's platform is usually taken for granted. However, there have been disagreements through the years. The last major one took place at the Democratic convention in 1948. After the party endorsed a plank backing civil rights reform, some of the conservative Democrats walked out of the convention. They formed the Dixiecrats (States' Rights Democrats) and ran Strom Thurmond of South Carolina for president. They carried four states, received thirty-nine electoral votes, and a popular vote of more than one million, but lost the election to Democrat Harry S. Truman.

Techniques and Advertising

As election time nears, the campaign team must decide how to get the party's message to the voting public, how to raise money, and how to get volunteers to help do both. The team stages rallies or public events to get attention. But that can backfire if no one comes! A mass meeting of the party faithful with a more-or-less prominent speaker draws people from outside the party. Volunteers get out the message by making phone calls or sending unsolicited e-mails. Sometimes people become annoyed with these techniques. People often object to being disturbed at mealtime or having their mailboxes stuffed with campaign messages. Whatever method they use, volunteers contact people and ask them to support the candidate or party, either by donating money or by volunteering their time.

In 1948, Republican Thomas Dewey challenged incumbent President Harry S. Truman for the White House. Truman had not been elected. As vice president in the administration of Franklin Roosevelt, he took office in 1945 after Roosevelt's death. All the public opinion polls pointed to Dewey as the winner in 1948. But Truman won, and his most famous photograph was taken on election day. The newly elected president is seen holding up the front page of the *Chicago Daily Tribune*. The headline reads: "Dewey Defeats Truman."

Truman had an interesting tactic to get out his message, which helped him pull off an upset victory. He organized an extensive railroad trip—called a whistlestop tour—from Iowa to California. The term *whistlestop tour* comes from train service in the early to mid–1940s, especially in the Midwest. Trains did not stop at small towns unless someone wanted to get off. The passenger who wanted to get off told the conductor, who signaled the engineer by pulling a cord. The engineer whistled back twice to say that he had received the message.

Truman's whistlestop train tour stopped as often as eight times a day (often in larger cities rather than in very small towns) so he could make speeches from a rear platform. When he got to Los Angeles he asked the crowd how they liked being referred to as a whistlestop. Apparently they did like it, because they cheered. Truman's political enemy, Senator Robert Taft of Ohio, had used a similar phrase by referring to "whistle stations," meaning small towns in the West. But Truman changed the term to whistlestop, and the name stuck.

The whistlestop tour was Truman's effective way of campaign advertising. Today the most important election technique in political advertising is the use of paid media. Television, radio, newspapers, the Internet, and other media forms get out the message and influence the vote. The ads that reach the public are generally designed by political consultants or members of the campaign staff. A number of tried-and-true marketing techniques have been effective—or sometimes backfired—through the years of political campaigning in America. They include the attack ad, the bumper sticker, the campaign button, canvassing, negative campaigning, and push polls.

The attack ad is a short—usually less than a minute—advertisement. It tries to smear a candidate's reputation, sometimes with humor, or it casts doubts on his or her ability to serve in office. A famous television attack ad—significant because it was a new use of political ads—appeared during the presidential campaign of 1964. Incumbent Lyndon B. Johnson was challenged by conservative Republican Barry Goldwater of Arizona. The Democratic campaign team ran a TV ad showing a young girl picking petals from a daisy. The camera zooms in on her eye, which fills the screen and blacks it out. The blackness turns to a flash and a mushroom cloud from a nuclear explosion. Called "Daisy Girl," the ad was meant to imply that Goldwater's harsh stand against the Soviet Union at the time could lead to nuclear war. The ad was effective, although Johnson's landslide victory was probably due to a sympathy vote. Johnson had been vice president during the administration of John F. Kennedy, who was killed by an assassin in 1963.

Another well-known attack ad was used successfully by the campaign team for George H. W. Bush in 1988. It

THIS PHOTOGRAPH SHOWING PRESIDENTIAL CANDIDATE MICHAEL DUKAKIS AS A TOUGH GUY IN A TANK BACKFIRED BADLY WHEN BUSH'S CAMPAIGN TEAM USED THE FOOTAGE IN AN ADVERTISEMENT.

showed pictures of Bush's Democratic opponent, Michael Dukakis, looking silly wearing a huge army attack helmet and riding in a tank. The ad probably helped defeat Dukakis. But another—and more effective—ad was based on the fact that, as governor of Massachusetts, Dukakis supported a weekend furlough program for convicted felons. The ad showed a convicted felon going through a revolving door to a prison. In 1987 William Horton—dubbed "Willie" by the Bush campaign—committed rape and armed robbery while on the weekend program.

In 2002 the Bipartisan Campaign Reform Act (also known as the McCain-Feingold law) was passed. Its main purpose was to reduce the influence of soft money in election campaigns, in effect reducing the power of rich donors. (Soft money is any contribution not regulated by federal election laws.) But it does not stop advocacy groups such as political action committees (PACs) from running attack ads. The 2006 Supreme Court decision in *Wisconsin Right to Life* v. *FEC* further reduced the restriction that McCain-Feingold intended for such groups. In the suit, Wisconsin Right to Life (WRTL) called itself a nonprofit advocacy corporation and sought to continue broadcasting its series of advertisements.

Bumper stickers and campaign buttons are well-known pieces of election advertising. The campaign team spends money to have drivers and pedestrians wear their candidates' names on buttons or clothing articles during the campaign. If the candidate loses, however, his or her face remains in defeat on many car bumpers. Campaign teams also give out lawn signs for the resident to advertise his or her favorite candidate.

Canvassing is a tedious but effective technique. It involves systematically targeting certain people in a group or in a particular area. It can be very effective, but it is also very time-consuming and requires very effective canvassers. It's necessary not only to know the group you want to target but also where they are. The idea may be to knock on doors to get Republicans to the polls. Therefore it's probably a waste of time to canvass an area known to be home to many labor union members, who usually vote Democratic. Door-to-door campaigning is known as field canvassing. Candidate canvassing involves sending the actual candidate, along with volunteers, to knock on doors. Phone canvasses reach a lot of people, since the message can be left on answering machines. The disadvantages are trying to get an up-to-date list of phone numbers and the annoyance that telemarketing engenders in many voters. Also, people can just delete messages left on their machines without listening.

Saying negative or mean things about an opponent has long been part of the democratic election process. It is often called mudslinging. The idea is to paint a picture of the opponent as somehow lacking, perhaps implying that he or she is soft on criminals or hasn't been honest on income tax returns. Such ads don't exactly come out and say that the opponent is not up to the demands of public office, but the implication is clear. When these negative campaign ads involve leaking damaging information to the media, they are known as dirty tricks. Sometimes the ads come from an outside source, hired by the campaign team. In the event that the ad backfires, the team can claim ignorance or that it was not responsible. A study in the *Political Science Review* in December 1999 found that negative ads do not seem to be more memorable than positive ones. There is also little evidence that such advertising lowers voter turnout. However, despite attempts to reduce or eliminate mudslinging, it remains part of the election process in more or less obvious degrees.

In 2006 Ted Brader published his findings concerning the emotional effects of political advertising in *Campaigning for Hearts and Minds*. After numerous experiments he concluded that an ad with emotional appeal is more likely to be remembered than one with logical appeal. Politically informed citizens are more likely to be influenced by emotional appeals than those who are less involved. Black-and-white videos generate fear or anger more than pride. Changing the music of a message while keeping the same text can produce an entirely different response. He concludes that, although politicians try to win both the hearts and the minds of voters, the heart is more likely to be won.

In the push poll campaign technique the party tries to influence votes by conducting a poll. This is generally seen as a form of negative advertising. It is condemned by the American Association of Political Consultants, a bipartisan group of political professionals. The technique involves making short telephone calls that are not aimed at obtaining information. The idea is to make a negative impression about the opposition candidate. A well-known use of a push poll reportedly occurred before the 2000 election when George W. Bush and Senator John McCain were running for the Republican nomination. Bush supporters called voters in South Carolina to ask if they would be more or less likely to vote for McCain if he had fathered an illegitimate black child. The question had no legitimacy (McCain and his wife had adopted a girl from Bangladesh). But political experts said it planted a negative thought in the minds of many voters.

3

The Money Trail: Who Pays?

No one can be elected president of the United States without spending a great deal of money. Not surprisingly, presidential campaigns become more expensive each year. Lincoln's campaign in 1860 cost about $100,000; Kennedy's race 100 years later cost about $9.7 million. Nixon ran up an impressive $61.4 million in 1972. And the price of reelecting George W. Bush in 2004 climbed to a staggering $200 million.

How do presidential campaigns raise funds? The issue of how to raise and spend money to become president has been around for a long, long time. But since 1976 every presidential election has been financed at least in part with public funds. However, the very early presidential candidates spent their own money or recruited someone else to donate to the campaign. The most costly expense was usually free whiskey that was handed out to voters on election day. In the 1800s there were added costs of parades and speeches at public rallies. Wealthy people were asked to contribute. The Democratic Party taxed the workers who

MONEY MAKES THE WORLD GO 'ROUND; IT'S ALSO ESSENTIAL TO SUCCESSFUL CAMPAIGNS. THIS NOT-SO-FANCIFUL IMAGE SHOWS ONE HUNDRED DOLLAR BILLS FLOATING ABOVE THE CAPITOL BUILDING.

owed their jobs to the party machine. By the early 1900s the excesses in fund-raising and unfair money-raising practices were obvious, so Congress passed the Tillman Act in 1907. It stopped banks and large companies from contributing to presidential and other candidates. But these and other congressional finance laws were often weakened by Supreme Court decisions.

In 1971 Congress passed the Federal Election Campaign Act (FECA). Along with the Revenue Act of 1971 it set up a system of laws and regulations regarding campaign money-raising and spending. However, it did not designate a single body to enforce the law. FECA said that contributions to campaigns as well as expenditures had to be fully reported. It also limited spending on media advertisements, but the Supreme Court later repealed those limits. FECA also built the framework for segregated funds, generally called PACs (political action committees). Unions and corporations set up PACs with treasury funds and ask for money from their workers. The money can then be donated to a presidential or other election campaign.

The Break-in at the Watergate

In 1974 Congress made major changes to the Federal Election Campaign Act of 1971. These changes were influenced by the Watergate scandal.

Today, any major—and even not so major—scandal is likely to have the suffix -*gate* added to it. That stems from the Watergate break-in that took place in the early 1970s. What seemed like a minor robbery turned into one of the biggest political controversies in U.S. history. It brought about the first resignation of a U.S. president. It also led to changes in the financing of political campaigns in the United States.

On June 17, 1972, five men were arrested for breaking into the headquarters of the Democratic National Committee at the Watergate complex in Washington, D.C. The arrested men were actually trying to fix a malfunctioning wiretap that they had installed earlier. One of the so-called burglars was a former CIA agent on the payroll of Richard Nixon's Committee to Re-Elect the President. Little by little, connections between the Watergate break-in and Nixon's reelection campaign grew stronger.

Despite Nixon's protests of ignorance, Watergate would not go away. Although he won his bid for reelection in November 1972, the investigation continued. On April 30, 1973, the president asked for the resignations of his top aides, H. R. Haldeman and John Ehrlichman.

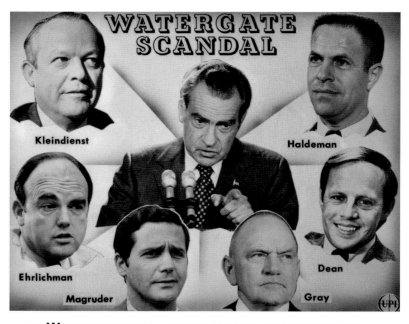

THE **WATERGATE** SCANDAL, WHICH LED TO THE IMPEACHMENT AND RESIGNATION OF **PRESIDENT RICHARD M. NIXON**, ALSO LED TO SIGNIFICANT CAMPAIGN REFORM.

(They would both eventually go to prison for their involvement in the scandal.) John Dean, counsel to the White House, was forced out. (He would eventually testify against Nixon.) By July 1973 the public was startled to learn that Nixon had a sophisticated taping system in the Oval Office. Everything that went on there was recorded. This news changed the focus of the investigation more pointedly toward the president's part in Watergate.

As Nixon continued to deny any knowledge of the break-in, protesters called for impeachment. When the public outcry grew louder, Nixon delivered a television speech on November 17, 1973. He proclaimed, "I am not a crook." But the steamroller continued. On July 27, 1974, the House Judiciary Committee voted 27 to 11 to recommend the first article of impeachment against Nixon.

With all support collapsing around him and with the Senate certain to convict, Richard Nixon resigned. He was pardoned by Gerald R. Ford, his vice president, who assumed the presidency when Nixon resigned. But the scandal of dirty campaigning plagued Nixon for the rest of his life. He died in 1994 at the age of eighty-one. Because of his association with the scandal, he was never again asked to appear at a national political convention, nor did he campaign for any candidate.

The news media were outraged at Nixon's pardon. However, Ford, who died in 2006, said that he felt it would help to heal the country's wounds. Political experts say the pardon was the main cause of Ford's loss to Jimmy Carter in the 1976 election.

Changes to Election Campaign Financing

Watergate was not the first—and is unlikely to be the last—political campaign scandal, but it was the one that was most blown out in the open. It led to charges of abuse

41

of power and obstruction of justice. Inquiries into Watergate revealed more than just a break-in. According to *Creative Campaigning*, "the inquiries revealed that President Nixon's fundraisers had accepted a number of extraordinarily large gifts, solicited illegal contributions from corporations, and attempted to secure donations by promising ambassadorial appointments, guaranteeing legislative favors, and offering other forms of undue influence."

Watergate left many lingering marks on the American political scene. The public still displays cynicism toward the press and sometimes the office of the president itself. The press has become more aggressive in reporting the misdeeds of politicians. Elections were conducted differently before and after the scandal of Watergate. For instance, it is now expected, if not legally required, that those in office release their income tax forms. And the practice of recording all Oval Office conversation has reportedly ended.

Watergate also led to tightened campaign financing practices. Before the scandal, election campaigns were mainly financed by corporations and small groups of wealthy donors. For instance, insurance executive W. Clement Stone contributed $2.8 million directly to Nixon's reelection campaign. In the wake of Watergate and increasing distrust from the voters, many members of Congress felt the need to limit the influence of such contributions.

In 1974 Congress made four changes to the Federal Election Campaign Act (FECA): (1) stricter rules for reporting campaign contributions and spending, (2) new limits on the amounts that can be spent for election, (3) limits to contributions to parties and candidates, and (4) creation of the Federal Election Commission (FEC).

The FEC is composed of six members appointed by the president and confirmed by the Senate. Each member serves a six-year term, and no more than three can be members of the same political party. The role of the FEC is limited to the administration of federal campaign finance laws. It keeps tabs on contributions and spending, investigates any possible violations, and administers the presidential campaign fund, which gives public money to qualified presidential candidates.

Key provisions of the 1974 amendments were immediately declared unconstitutional. The lawsuit was filed by two former senators, Republican James L. Buckley of New York and Democrat Eugene McCarthy of Minnesota. As a result the Supreme Court ruled that contribution limits were constitutional because they helped keep the elections fair. But the Court overturned the expenditure limits. It also made some changes in the method of appointing FEC commissioners; originally, Congress appointed four members.

According to current election finance laws, qualified candidates can apply for public matching funds. Up to certain limits, private individual contributions to the candidate and party are matched by government money. The candidates of the major parties can receive a public grant to finance the general election, as long as they do not use private funds. In 2004 the grant to the major parties was about $75 million each. The government also contributes public funds for the cost of the Democratic and Republican national conventions before each presidential election. The minor parties can also receive some money for conventions, provided that their candidates got more than 5 percent of the vote in the previous presidential election.

Individuals can contribute no more than two thousand dollars to a presidential candidate election. Thousands of Americans give money in smaller amounts to the candidates they want to put into office. Political action committees can contribute no more than five thousand dollars per candidate per election. The largest contributions to candidates come from companies and industries. In 1978 a federal funding law created a loophole that opened the door for the use of so-called soft money. The Republican Party, more of a friend to large companies than the Democrats, benefits the most from this soft money loophole. For instance, in the 2000 election, oil and gas companies contributed $345 million to the campaigns. Of that, about 79 percent went to the Republican candidates. Republicans generally benefit more from soft money because their contributors are generally richer than those who give to the Democrats.

Congress tried to close the soft money loophole by limiting such contributions. The Bipartisan Campaign Reform Act (BCRA) of 2002 set new spending limits on soft money contributions to national political parties. Typical soft money contributions come from large business corporations that generally give soft money to Republicans, or labor unions that generally donate to the Democrats. Soft money donations are known as indirect funds. Hard money donations are direct contributions to a candidate from individuals and organizations, such as a political action committee or political party. The donations must be declared in the name of the donor and become public knowledge.

The overriding goal of BCRA is to limit the influence of large donors on election campaigns. But it has also banned supposedly nonpartisan issue ads. A wealthy person, for instance, might donate $10 million to the Republican Party. The party spends the money on ads. Such ads might try to assassinate the character of the opposing candidate. For instance, in 2003, Howard Dean was the front-runner at one point in his campaign for the Democratic nomination. Ads began to appear criticizing Dean

What About Third Parties?

Seemingly lost in the scramble for campaign money are the third parties. Actually, third-party candidates are also eligible for public funding. They get less money than the major parties, however, because they have a lower percentage of voters. In order to qualify for funding, a third-party candidate must have totaled between 5 and 25 percent of the popular vote in the previous presidential election. More than 25 percent turns the third party into a major party, which is then under the same rules as the Democrats and Republicans. If the third party had no candidate in the previous election, it will get public money once the election is over if its candidate receives at least 5 percent of the vote.

about his record on gun rights and Medicare. Visuals of known terrorists popped up, which seemed to question Dean's knowledge of foreign policy. The smear tactics were effective and may be a major reason that Dean lost the nomination to John Kerry. The ads were paid for by the Americans for Jobs & Healthcare; later disclosures indicated that the group contributed to Kerry's campaign. According to the Center for Public Integrity, "In the twenty-first century in the United States of America, it is still astonishingly easy to assassinate a political opponent's character. It is hardly new to politics anywhere that money and the messages it buys often create devastating perceptions. But such smear tactics are more serious and offensive when they benefit major 'mainstream' candidates seeking the Presidency." BCRA tried to limit the effect of such ads by requiring a candidate to endorse them.

However, in a June 2007 ruling, the Supreme Court weakened the curbs that BCRA tried to impose. The Court said that to prohibit the use of a candidate's name in a pre-election ad was an infringement of the group's rights to voice its opinion on issues.

There is also controversy over so-called 527 groups, tax-exempt organizations that are named after a section of the U.S. tax code. The purpose of a 527 group is mainly to influence the election or defeat of candidates. The groups are run by special interest groups, and they are not regulated by the FEC. These groups can raise unlimited amounts of money, and their influence is substantial. In April 2004 the FEC decided that campaign finance laws did not cover 527s unless they *directly* called for the election or defeat of a candidate. Congress is currently considering placing new limits on these groups.

Why do corporations, groups, and people contribute money to election campaigns? The simple and complicated answer is influence. Individuals may want a certain person in office who might favor certain legislation. That is true

ONE ASPECT OF CAMPAIGN REFORM WAS TO REQUIRE CANDIDATES TO TAKE RESPONSIBILITY FOR THEIR ADVERTISEMENTS IN AN ATTEMPT TO LIMIT THE SMEARS. (ABOVE) AN ADVERTISEMENT APPROVED BY JOHN KERRY IN THE 2000 PRESIDENTIAL CAMPAIGN CRITICIZES GEORGE W. BUSH FOR RUNNING A SMEAR CAMPAIGN. (BELOW) THIS AD APPROVED BY PRESIDENT BUSH QUESTIONS JOHN KERRY'S CHARACTER.

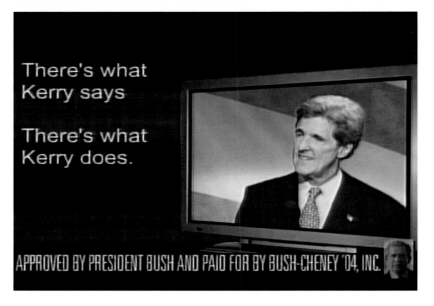

of big companies as well. A candidate who is known to favor limited regulation of oil companies, for instance, will be helped by soft money contributions from those industries. Despite the many federal regulations that exist, these contributions are legal. Do they work? As Warren Buffett, the second wealthiest man in the United States, said, "Corporations think they are getting their money's worth or they wouldn't be writing checks."

In his 2004 bid for the Democratic presidential nomination, Howard Dean used a new tactic: the Internet. Dean's was the first presidential campaign known to have a blog. (A blog is a personal Web site set up much like a list or diary, with the most recent entry at the top.) And it worked—to a point. By using the Internet to get his message across, Dean went from an obscure Vermont governor to a viable candidate. He raised a record $7.5 million, mostly from small donations, in a second-quarter fund-raising blitz. (Hillary Clinton broke Dean's record when she raised $26 million during the first quarter of 2007 in her bid for the Democratic presidential nomination.) But the Internet went just so far; Dean lost the nomination to Kerry.

Finance Reform: The Debate Goes On

The government has long been trying to regulate and reform the financing of presidential campaigns. There is still much debate over limits on campaign contributions and spending. Those who are against limits or are for raising them have many arguments. An individual contribution of two thousand dollars is not worth as much as it was years ago, so more money is needed to help a candidate win. Higher contribution limits might help candidates who are challenging incumbents to get their campaigns rolling. With higher limits candidates could spend less time raising funds and more time explaining their stand to the people. The increasing cost of TV advertising, which is so important to modern campaigns, makes higher limits essential for candidates to get out their messages.

Those who want to limit campaign spending disagree. They say that few individuals can afford to give two thousand dollars to a campaign. Increasing the campaign limit or taking it away would mean that rich people and other individual contributors would have more influence than ever. They claim that lifting the limits would not give challengers an easier task of raising money, since wealthy contributors generally favor the incumbents. Adding more money would not solve the current financial problems. Wealthy people who are not limited by current finance laws—soft money—will continue to spend it. Higher limits will become as easy to evade legally as current ones.

No one on either side of current U.S. laws on campaign election spending is satisfied. One proposed system for change is called clean elections or clean money. So far it operates at the state level in Arizona, Connecticut, Maine, New Jersey, New Mexico, North Carolina, and Vermont. Under this system, candidates who want public financing first have to collect a certain number (determined by each state) of small (as little as five dollars) contributions from registered voters. They agree to accept a small amount of private money (the amount varies by state), and the government then gives the candidates a flat sum (which also varies by state). The clean election candidate who is outspent by a privately funded candidate can receive matching government money. This type of campaign financing has had some success, but is opposed by huge industry giants such as drug and insurance companies.

There are other proposals for change as well. A candidate might be allowed to raise money from private donors with matching funds from the first chunk of the donations. For example the government might match the first two hundred dollars of each donation. Other states have some form of limited financial assistance for candidates.

Any changes to campaign finance reform have critics. Some say that such reform violates First Amendment rights. If political advertising is restricted, then that conflicts with the right of freedom of political speech. Others argue that reform discourages participation in the election process. Some say that more and more rules will discourage people from running for public office, which will make elections less competitive.

Is too much money spent on U.S. election campaigns? And is all that spending bad for democracy? Considering all the arguments about campaign reform, the answers would seem to be yes. But not all experts think so. In a 2004 article entitled "Why Is There So Little Money in U.S. Politics?" in the *Journal of Economic Perspectives*, Stephen Ansolabehere and his coauthors argue that most campaign contributions come from individuals who want to participate in the election process, not buy it. They claim that most studies do not support the idea that contributions buy votes. And they see giving money to campaigns, which they say is generally dependent on income, as good and normal for the country.

4

The Multibillion-Dollar Industry

Political campaigns in the United States are a multibillion-dollar industry. Just based on their length, that should not be surprising. Compared to elections in other countries, such as the United Kingdom, U.S. presidential races are a marathon. For instance, 2007 had hardly begun when news broadcasters were already discussing the presidential tickets for November 2008! And 2007 marked the earliest beginning for a presidential race in U.S. history. Former vice-presidential candidate John Edwards announced his candidacy at the end of December 2006. Senators Hillary Clinton and Barack Obama entered the race for the Democratic nomination the following February. They were soon joined by a number of other contenders from both parties.

Throughout U.S. history, presidential campaigns have resulted in some fascinating races as well as some strange happenings after the cheering was over. For instance, in the election of 1840, winner William Henry Harrison of Ohio had the sad distinction of serving the shortest presidential term in U.S. history. That election was the first time that two political parties organized on a grand scale, with the Whigs (Harrison's party) against Democrat Martin Van Buren. Harrison won mainly because he was known as the hero of the Battle of Tippecanoe, where he defeated the Shawnee in 1811. His campaign slogan was "Tippecanoe and Tyler Too!" Harrison won with 53 percent of the vote and gave a very long inaugural speech. He stood bareheaded in the cold and rain on March 4, 1841. At age sixty-eight he was the oldest man yet to serve in the White House. But he caught a cold and died on April 4. His running mate, John Tyler of Virginia, became president.

Republican James A. Garfield was the second president—after Lincoln—to be assassinated. He was in the railroad station on the morning of July 2, 1881, when Charles J. Guiteau, a mentally disturbed man, shot Garfield in the arm and back. Surgeons could not remove the bullet, and he died on September 19 at the age of fifty. Guiteau was hanged.

For a strange turnabout in American presidential campaigns and elections, it is hard to beat the Hayes-Tilden race of 1876. Some call it a blatant misuse of power. Republican Rutherford B. Hayes of Ohio ran against New York Governor Samuel Jones Tilden, a Democrat. The campaign was ugly, with both sides accusing one another of misdeeds. The morning after the election, it was clear that Tilden had won, with 203 electoral votes against 166 for Hayes. The popular vote was close, however, and the Republicans saw a way to victory. They demanded recounts in various states, charging that African Americans had been denied the vote. The battle went on for three months. Finally it was decided to create a special fifteen-man Electoral Commission—seven Republicans, seven Democrats, and one Independent—to settle the dispute. Just before voting, the Independent, a Supreme Court justice, resigned from the Commission to accept a seat in

THIS 1876 CARTOON BY THOMAS NAST SHOWS THE BALLOT BOX BEING KICKED AROUND LIKE A POLITICAL FOOTBALL DURING THE DISPUTED HAYES-TILDEN ELECTION.

the Senate. Since there were more Republicans than Democrats on the Court the justices, not surprisingly, chose a Republican to replace the Independent. Also not surprisingly, the Commission voted along party lines, giving Hayes the election, 8 to 7. He became the nation's nineteenth president just fifty-six hours before the scheduled inauguration ceremony.

The Primary and Caucus

Before anyone can vote in an election, there must be candidates to vote for. Aside from needing money, how does a person get to run for president of the United States? Who chooses which candidates will be on the presidential ticket in an election year?

After political parties entered the U.S. election scene late in the eighteenth century, candidates were chosen by a meeting of party members, usually without state regulation. Party leaders could, therefore, select their candidates by almost any method they chose. This led to the so-called smoke-filled back rooms. There, it is said, the heads of the parties pleaded, threatened, or arm-twisted behind closed doors to get their candidate nominated.

Since the 1920s, however, candidates for president and other offices have mainly been chosen in state primaries or caucuses. The process may be more fair, but it is often far more confusing. Before the presidential election of 2008 Democrats and Republicans held about one hundred meetings in the fifty states, the District of Columbia, and Puerto Rico to elect candidates for that November.

These state meetings are called primaries or caucuses. A primary is an election in a certain district, such as a state, held prior to the national election. The most common primaries are open or closed. In an open primary citizens can vote in a party's primary even if they are not registered with that party. In a closed primary voters must be registered with the party in order to vote.

Other systems include the blanket primary, also called a jungle primary, in which a voter may select one candidate for each office without regard to party lines. For example, the voter might select a Democrat for the Senate and a Republican for governor. The candidates with the highest votes for each office go to the general election. An

Primaries by State

Closed: Arizona, California, Colorado, Connecticut, Delaware, District of Columbia, Florida, Kansas, Kentucky, Maine, Maryland, Massachusetts, Nebraska, Nevada, New Hampshire, New Jersey, New Mexico, New York, North Carolina, Oklahoma, Oregon, Pennsylvania, Rhode Island, South Dakota, Utah, West Virginia, Wyoming

Open: Alabama, Arkansas, Georgia, Hawaii, Idaho, Indiana, Michigan, Minnesota, Mississippi, Missouri, Montana, North Dakota, South Carolina, Tennessee, Texas, Vermont, Virginia, Washington, Wisconsin

Other: Alaska: Blanket primary for four of the five registered parties; Republicans have closed primary. Illinois and Ohio: Must vote in the primary of the same party as the last primary vote, loosely enforced. Iowa: Voter may change registration at polls. Louisiana: Top two runoff system; closed primary for congressional races after 2006.

instant runoff voting (IRV) system is used for single-member elections in which each voter has one vote but can choose candidates in order of preference. If no candidate gets the majority of first choices, those with the fewest numbers of votes are excluded one by one. Those votes are given to the next candidate, according to the voter's preference. The process is repeated until one candidate gets a majority.

The large majority of states hold primaries, but a few choose the caucus. This is a meeting of voters at the precinct level, which is the smallest electoral district in the country. Caucuses are generally set at the same time throughout the state.

Contrary to the impression given by media coverage, the main purpose of both primaries and caucuses is not to choose a presidential candidate. The purpose is to select delegates from each party to go to that party's national convention held in the summer before the November election. In some primaries, voters check a presidential candidate's name. But they are actually voting for a delegate who pledges to go to the convention in support of that candidate.

The small state of New Hampshire has been big news for all of the presidential elections since 1977. It long held the nation's first presidential primary, which was regarded as influential for the election. That did not always prove to be true, however. Pat Buchanan won the New Hampshire primary in 1996, but Bob Dole became the Republican candidate. John McCain took the Republican New Hampshire primary by 19 points in 2000, but George W. Bush got the nomination. New Hampshire has long taken pride in having the first primary. State law says that New Hampshire's primary must be held at least a week before any other state's. That does not include the caucus. Iowa usually has its caucus before New Hampshire's primary.

However, New Hampshire is being challenged as the state to hold the first primary. The challenge is affecting the way candidates campaign for office. Since the 2000 election many states are moving up their primaries to get the first spotlight. That means that more and more potential candidates declare their intentions earlier in order to enter the early primaries to get name recognition. That means money must be raised and candidates must get out their messages far earlier than ever. If the trend continues the national conventions will be merely window dressing —as they almost are now. By gaining votes in the primaries a candidate may sew up the nomination even before the first convention speech.

At various times there have been suggestions for reforming the long and costly primary system. A single nationwide primary has been suggested. The American Plan calls for a more relaxed schedule with fewer primaries in the smaller states. The Republican National Committee in 2000 recommended the Delaware Plan, which tried to stop the states from scheduling their primaries earlier and earlier. No reform plan has been passed.

The Convention

The primaries and the caucuses are over. The delegates are chosen. Now comes the process known as the political convention. Today there is rarely any suspense about the choice of candidates. A guide to the electoral process by the League of Women Voters says, "It used to be that conventions could easily turn into high-drama affairs as the parties battled within themselves over key issues, and the selection of the party's nominees for president and vice president wasn't certain until the final voting. But today, the conventions have turned into what one television anchor has called infomercials for the national parties.

The Forgotten Candidate

Until recent decades, generally little attention was paid to the nomination of the vice president at the convention. Sometimes the presidential nominee named his choice. The position was usually used to balance the ticket; if the presidential candidate came from the northeast, the vice president might come from the southwest. In general the position of vice president was not highly regarded or sought after. John Adams, the first vice president, often complained that the job was boring. However, since the assassination of John Kennedy and the resignation of Richard Nixon, the position of vice president is looked on more seriously as a possible stepping-stone to the highest office.

They are events that are scripted with one thing in mind: marketing the party and its candidates to the American electorate."

Gone are the days when the political convention was a grand spectacle for all. The greatest show occurred when the nominee was in doubt and needed a certain number of votes to get on the ticket. An announcement of each state's choice began in alphabetical order. As the tally grew closer, one state had the honor of reaching the required number of votes to name the candidate. With great drama the state's delegate took the microphone and usually began a long string of compliments about the state itself. Then he or she said the magic words: "The great state of X casts its (number of) votes for Y." On cue millions of balloons headed for the ceiling, several bands struck up a rousing tune, and delegates marched around the convention hall amid cheers and much flag waving. It is a scene that has largely vanished.

The first of what became these grand spectacles was held, oddly enough, by a third party, the Anti-Masons, in 1831. The Republicans and Democrats soon followed. The gatherings grew in size and fanfare, with the nomination usually still up for grabs. But by the mid–1900s the news and television coverage of primaries began to play a larger and larger role. In the 1960 election there were misgivings about Kennedy's ability to win because he was a Catholic. But he went into the Democratic convention with wins in all seven primaries, thereby proving that a Catholic could get Protestant votes. He was elected on the first ballot at the convention.

Over the years since Kennedy's convention, the parties have moved from a convention-centered to a primary-centered nominating system. Greater media coverage that begins shortly after a primary election makes the convention itself less crucial to the actual nomination. Today a

Some Memorable Political Conventions

Through the years political conventions have presented the highs and lows of American politics:

In Baltimore in 1860, the Democratic Party agreed that the Supreme Court should make the decisions on slavery. Delegates from several Southern states walked out and formed the Southern Democratic Party.

In Chicago, abolitionist Frederick Douglass became the first African American to receive a vote (just one) at a political (Republican) convention after the Civil War.

The Democratic convention in Chicago in 1968 was a scene of televised violence in the streets and shouting on the convention floor. Anti–Vietnam War groups protested. Police, under the tight control of Chicago Mayor Richard Daley, fought some ten thousand protesters with tear gas and riot gear. In the end, war supporter Hubert Humphrey got the nomination over anti-war candidate Eugene McCarthy.

On the night of George McGovern's acceptance speech at the 1972 Democratic convention in Miami Beach, Florida, there was so much dispute over issues that he didn't get to the microphone until the early morning hours. By that time most of the country had gone to bed and never heard him. He lost the general election to Nixon.

At the 2000 Democratic convention in Los Angeles, a performance by the politically active rock group Rage Against the Machine was stopped by police. They fought the spectators with pepper spray and rubber bullets.

For the first time in history the Republicans held their convention in New York City, not known for being friendly to their party. But in 2004, New York had a Republican mayor and it seemed politically wise to support the Big Apple, which had suffered most from the terrorist attacks of 9/11. As it turned out, about 1,800 demonstrators were arrested.

first-ballot nomination at a convention simply may not be needed. Primaries are held earlier and earlier. They are covered extensively by television and other media. The voting results are known as they happen. Therefore a candidate can go into the convention, and even into later primaries, with the nomination already in his or her pocket. Behind-the-scenes party work may go on at the convention, but the politicking that once led to a nomination is about to become a thing of the past.

If there is little suspense concerning the presidential candidate by convention time, many political leaders like it that way. Surprises are not what politicians usually want at conventions. As the 1996 convention neared, with Clinton certain to be renominated, Democratic consultant James Carville said, "Boring is good."

In effect, in the twenty-first century, the political convention has gone from being a way of selecting a candidate to a way of showing off his or her talents. It is also a showcase for party image. Each party selects convention speakers who will appeal to the public and present the platform in its most "vote-able" form. That doesn't always work, however. At the 1992 Republican convention to reelect George H. W. Bush, one of the speakers was conservative Pat Buchanan, who had challenged Bush for the nomination. Buchanan spent most of his speech focusing on his own beliefs and those of his followers, and little on Bush. The authors of *Political Parties, Interest Groups, and Political Campaigns* noted, "Although controversy over the Buchanan speech probably did not contribute to Bush's defeat, it certainly did not help the Bush-Quayle ticket focus attention on the themes they wanted to communicate to voters."

In whatever form they take, political conventions do give the candidates what is called a bounce. A candidate's approval rating with the public usually jumps right after

CONVENTIONS ARE HELD TO NOMINATE CANDIDATES, BUT THEY ARE SOMETIMES ALSO OCCASIONS FOR PROTESTORS TO MAKE THEIR FEELINGS HEARD. ON AUGUST 29, 2004, HUNDREDS OF THOUSANDS OF PEOPLE MARCHED TOWARD THE SITE OF THE REPUBLICAN NATIONAL CONVENTION IN NEW YORK TO PROTEST AGAINST THE WAR IN IRAQ AND THE BUSH ADMINISTRATION'S DOMESTIC POLICIES.

the nomination. After the 2004 Democratic convention, John Kerry got a four-point bounce in the polls. But the Republican convention soon followed, and George Bush emerged with an eleven-point lead over Kerry.

Political conventions in the twenty-first century may not be as exciting as they once were, but they do follow the old rules on certain key events. The keynote address rallies the party faithful around main issues. It is usually delivered by an up-and-coming party member. The party platform, which highlights what the party stands for, is adopted. The candidates for president and vice president are formally nominated. Usually longest of all is the presidential candidate's acceptance speech. From there the delegates and candidates begin the real work of getting out the vote in November.

5
Informing the Public
. . . or Not

A century or more ago, election news might take a long time to reach most Americans. Today almost no one is out of the media's reach. Most Americans get all their information and news about candidates, the political parties, and election issues from radio, newspapers, news magazines, and, most of all, the Internet and television. The use of television changed the whole nature of the presidency and presidential campaigning. And it began with the 1960 debates between Republican Richard M. Nixon, a two-term vice president, and Democrat John F. Kennedy, a three-term representative and senator since 1953, in their race for the White House.

The four debates between September 26 and October 21 marked television's grand entrance into presidential politics. It has been there ever since. The two candidates discussed domestic issues, U.S. involvement with islands off the coast of China, and relations with Cuba. They were evenly matched in facts, but the difference in physical appearance was striking. Nixon had been in the hospital for a knee injury shortly before the debates. He had lost

JOHN F. KENNEDY'S UNDERSTANDING OF THE TELEVISION CAMERA PLAYED A LARGE PART IN HIS ELECTION TO THE PRESIDENCY IN 1960. THOSE WHO LISTENED TO HIS DEBATE WITH RICHARD NIXON ON THE RADIO THOUGHT THE LATTER HAD WON; THOSE WHO SAW THE DEBATE GAVE THE VICTORY TO KENNEDY, HANDS DOWN.

weight, his complexion was pale, and—because he refused the usual TV makeup—he looked unshaven. Kennedy, on the other hand, was tan and healthy-looking.

In an article entitled "The Great Debate," history professor Liette Gidlow says, "The debates made Kennedy look like a winner." His practice of looking into the television camera instead of at the journalist who asked a question made viewers feel as though he were talking directly to them. Gidlow noted that "polls taken after the debate showed that most people who listened to it on the radio felt that Nixon had won, while most who watched it on television declared Kennedy the winner." The election was very close, and Kennedy might have won without television, but it certainly helped.

In fact, since then, campaigners must pass the television test. Is he wearing a hairpiece? Is it true that she has had Botox injections? Do they dye their hair? In addition to other media forms, Americans increasingly get their information about candidates from blogs and from shows hosted by comedians and political satirists such as Jon Stewart. These TV shows often feature guest appearances by the candidates. It is still not certain whether television exposure alone can sway an election, but there is little doubt that in the twenty-first century the TV screen plays a big part in choosing who will sit in the White House.

Fair or Biased Reporting?

Although few argue that the media have a role to play in U.S. political campaigns, many disagree about what that role should be and how it should be conducted. It seems obvious that campaigns should be covered fairly. But the media have often been criticized for the ways in which they affect campaigns and elections. Among the criticisms are too much focus on a candidate's personality rather than what he or she stands for; too many sound bites, short items that don't say anything of substance; too much focus on scandals; too much so-called news coverage, especially on television, that is really not news at all, but instead is more a personality or lifestyle review.

Newspapers often earn reputations based on their stands on political issues. The *New York Times*, for instance, is known as a liberal publication, as are the *Washington Post* and *St. Louis Dispatch*, among others. Conservative papers include the *New York Post* since it was bought by Rupert Murdoch. For a long time the highly conservative *Manchester Union Leader* in New Hampshire was brazen about promoting the candidates it liked and running down those it didn't. According to author Rhodes Cook, "In a scathing vernacular that reflected the paper's longtime publisher, William Loeb, Dwight Eisenhower was 'Dopey Dwight.'" New York governor Nelson Rockefeller and Massachusetts senator Edward Kennedy were also described in unflattering terms. On the other hand, the *Union Leader* described Pat Buchanan, whom the paper endorsed in the 1992 Republican primary over President George Bush, as the "Most Honorable of Men."

One of the worst aspects of newspaper coverage was so-called yellow journalism. It involved publisher William Randolph Hearst of the *New York Journal*. Hearst and Joseph Pulitzer, publisher of the *New York World*, would apparently stop at nothing in their competition to beat each other. That included a certain disregard for the truth. Yellow journalism is the printing of distorted stories or sensational headlines without facts to back them. Especially in the late nineteenth and early twentieth centuries, newspapers used yellow journalism to boost circulation and destroy opposition candidates. Few newspapers might admit it, but yellow journalism continues today, although perhaps in a more refined manner. At times there may be an "anything goes" attitude in reporting to the public, but overt bias in political reporting has been around for a long time. Blaring headlines and the depth or paucity of coverage can remind readers always to be aware of the validity of their news sources.

In response to criticisms of biased reporting, some major newspapers say that they do check on the truth of election TV and radio ads by candidates. *USA Today*, for instance, runs so-called ad watches that analyze election statements. Some cable networks give free air time for candidates to state their positions on issues, although this is not a general practice. The growth of cable news networks has expanded the range of information that is open to voters. It also allows networks to deliver their own commentary. The FOX network, for instance, delivers both news and commentary with a distinctly conservative flavor, even though it declares itself to be evenhanded.

The Internet is becoming an enormous factor in campaign financing and presidential elections. In the presidential debate between Bob Dole and Clinton in 1996, Dole mentioned his Web site. So many people checked it that the server was overloaded and had to shut down. When

THE INTERNET HAS CREATED A NEW FORUM FOR POLITICAL CAMPAIGNS. JOAN BLADES, MOVEON.ORG COFOUNDER, DISPLAYS TWO POLITICAL ADS THE ORGANIZATION RAN ON THE INTERNET DURING THE 2004 CAMPAIGN: A PHOTO OF A GIRL HOLDING A DAISY THAT CHANGES INTO AN IMAGE OF THE AFTERMATH OF NUCLEAR DESTRUCTION—FIRST MADE FAMOUS WHEN LYNDON BAINES JOHNSON RAN SUCCESSFULLY AGAINST BARRY GOLDWATER IN 1964—AND AN ANTI–IRAQ WAR ADVERTISEMENT TARGETING THE BUSH ADMINISTRATION.

Hillary Clinton began her run for the Democratic nomination in early 2007, she did so first on her Web site instead of announcing it on TV.

There is little doubt that Web sites and other Internet uses will offer the public more campaign information than ever before. DemocracyNet (http://www.dnet.org), created by the League of Women Voters, is a nonpartisan election resource. Both the Democratic and Republican National Committees have official Web sites with data on candidates, issues, party platforms, and conventions. Rock the Vote (www.rockthevote.org) is a Web site that covers elections and voting and is slanted toward teens. MoveOn.org considers itself a nonprofit organization focused on education and advocacy of national issues in a fight for a progressive America. In all cases, the problem for the voter is still how to tell what is hype from what is fact.

The power of the media can influence voter decisions and presidential elections. Through the years the media have been instrumental in bringing the facts to the public, as in the Watergate scandal. At times administrations have been skillful in withholding or disguising any potentially damaging news—that is, news that might be damaging for the party or the next election. The media have also joined a sitting administration in keeping secrets from the rest of the country.

Roosevelt: The Polio That Wasn't There

Members of the press, unlike most of the rest of the country, were aware that Franklin Delano Roosevelt, the thirty-second president of the United States (1933–1945), could not walk unaided. In fact, as stated in *FDR's Splendid Deception*, "Franklin Delano Roosevelt was the only person in the recorded history of mankind who was chosen as a leader by his people even though he could not walk or stand without help." In fact, he was chosen four times. Many people who grew up under Roosevelt's leadership now say that they were unaware of his condition at the time. Others say that they knew FDR had contracted polio years earlier but thought he suffered only from a slight limp. The Roosevelt administration and the Secret Service kept his disability a tight secret, and the media helped. Even at his campaign speech at his last election, literally surrounded by supporters, Roosevelt appeared to walk to the platform even though he was actually supported by aides.

Roosevelt—a Democrat—was the first and only president to be elected to four terms. After his death the newly Republican Congress wanted to make sure that presidents could not be elected more than twice. The rationale was that the position could become a dictatorship and much too powerful. The Twenty-Second Amendment to the Constitution, ratified in 1951, limits presidents to two terms. There has been some limited debate through the years over this amendment. Some people argue that it unfairly restricts a person's ability to win the vote.

The son of a wealthy railroad executive, Roosevelt entered politics at the age of twenty-eight when he became a state assemblyman in New York. He was the vice-presidential candidate on the 1920 Democratic ticket, but the Republicans won, with Warren G. Harding becoming president.

The following summer Roosevelt, at age thirty-nine, was vacationing with his family at their summer home on Campobello Island in Canada. He developed a chill and fever. Two days later he could not walk. He would never again walk without aid. Roosevelt had contracted poliomyelitis, or polio, which was then more generally known as infantile paralysis. It was a dreadfully feared and crippling disease until Jonas Salk virtually wiped it out with the vaccine he developed in 1952.

After becoming ill Roosevelt spent the next seven years trying to recover at Warm Springs, Georgia. He then re-entered politics and was elected president of the United States in 1932, serving until his death from a cerebral hemorrhage in April 1945. He is credited with bringing the country out of the Great Depression and with guiding it to victory in World War II.

During all that time the reason few people in the country were aware that the president could not walk or stand unaided was because Roosevelt's public life was well choreographed. As noted in "Roosevelt: A Presidential Campaign," "He never appeared paralyzed. Whenever he was in public, he would lock his leg braces at the knees, so that his legs would not collapse. He would lean on canes or someone's arm. He never allowed himself to be photographed by the media in a wheelchair or while he was being carried. When he was photographed, he was shown sitting behind a desk or in a car, or leaning against a railing as he delivered a speech with eloquence and passion. He even painted his crutches to match his socks. . . . Only two known photographs exist of Roosevelt in his wheelchair."

And the media cooperated. A conscious if unspoken decision was made among members of the press to keep the president's disability from the public. That may seem amazing today, in light of the scrutiny by TV cameras. But the media for the most part did aid in what may be called a political deception. Roosevelt's condition was even kept out of the international media. When he met with Winston Churchill and Joseph Stalin to discuss peace terms in 1945, he was never shown in a wheelchair. Part of the reason for this political deception was the feeling that the country needed strength to get through World War II. It was thought, rightly or wrongly—including by Roosevelt himself—the nation must be assured that a strong leader was in charge. That presumably meant one who could stand on two feet.

There is still debate over the issue of the press withholding information from the public. Some argue that, in the case of Roosevelt, the war climate was such that the appearance of a physically strong leader was important to the nation's morale. Others argue that deceit is morally wrong whatever the situation.

The Media and Presidential Scandals

The media and presidential scandals are not strangers. When a sitting president becomes involved in a scandal it is always big news. After the Kennedy assassination in 1963 many stories circulated about his romances with movie stars such as Marilyn Monroe and secret liaisons at the White House. These had been covered up—or ignored—by the press, whose members generally liked Kennedy. The issue of reporting everything is still debated today. Some people feel that what goes on behind closed doors is not the business of the press or the public. Some say that, although the focus should be on public performance, for those who put themselves in the public eye, anything they do is fair game.

In many instances when a politician does something that might be of interest to the press, the real truth remains secret, at least until the person in question dies. That was not the case, however, with Bill Clinton, the forty-second president (1993–2001). Society often judges a leader harshly if his or her behavior is thought to be inappropriate. Sometimes, however, what is or is not considered appropriate can change.

In January 1998 the *Washington Post* ran a story

about a supposed relationship between Clinton and Monica Lewinsky, an intern who worked at the White House during his first term. Clinton vehemently denied any involvement with Lewinsky in a televised conference. But the rumors swirled and the press kept the story alive. In grand jury testimony in April of that year, Clinton admitted that his behavior was—as he termed it—inappropriate and that he had lied. In early December, the House of Representatives started impeachment proceedings on two counts: perjury before a grand jury and obstruction of justice. The case was sent to the Senate in January 1999.

The Senate voted not guilty on both counts, the vote largely along party lines. Therefore the president was impeached, contrary to a popular misconception. To be impeached meant that the House sent the case to be tried by the Senate, which it did. He was not convicted. That is why Clinton stayed in office and had no penalty, except for House censure.

But how much effect did the impeachment have on Clinton's reelection? Apparently little. He was reelected in 1996, beating Republican Senator Robert Dole with 49 percent of the popular vote and 379 electoral votes compared with Dole's 159. U.S. voters may not have condoned Clinton's behavior, but they also felt that Republicans were hypocritical in the way they pressed for impeachment. In fact Republicans made Clinton's extramarital conduct a major issue in the congressional elections two years later and almost lost control of the House as a result.

6

Challenging the Vote

The United States is a federal republic. It is composed of self-governing states united by a federal government. The people hold the ruling power either directly or through elected representatives. In other words, the people vote.

But not everyone can or does vote. A qualified voter must be born in the United States or naturalized, meaning that he or she has become a U.S. citizen. Voters must be at least eighteen years old, and they must be registered. Registration forms can be obtained at various sites, such as libraries, voter registration offices, and online. The form can be mailed to the address listed on the form, and the voter will receive a registration card in the mail. Generally, convicted felons and those judged mentally incompetent are excluded from voting. State voter registration also differs concerning how long the voter needs to have lived there. However, from the beginning of U.S. history and continuing today, states use registration practices to discriminate against voters and influence the outcome of elections.

The Thirteenth Amendment (1865) ended slavery in the United States. The Fourteenth Amendment (1868) said that all those born in the United States, including African Americans, are natural citizens. The Fifteenth Amendment (1870) declared that no one can be denied the right to vote because of race or color or having once been a slave. These three amendments should assure voting rights to African Americans. But that has not been the case. Years after the Civil War when federal troops pulled out of many Southern states, African Americans in large numbers were barred from voting. Threats of violence as well as actual violence kept thousands from the polls. So did the requirement that a voter must be able to read and write. Most slaves were not allowed to learn to read and write, so of course they could not pass that voter qualification rule in the years following the Thirteenth and Fourteenth amendments. And even those who were literate were barred from the polls by various means because of their skin color. It took nearly another century and the passage of the Voting Rights Act of 1965 to help strike down discrimination in the voting booth.

Civil Rights and Presidential Campaigns

The beginning of the modern civil rights movement to end discrimination in the United States is usually dated to December 1, 1955. On that day Rosa Parks refused to give up her seat on the bus to a white person as required by the laws of Montgomery, Alabama. She later said she was just tired. But Parks was not merely the quiet seamstress she seemed to be. Educated at Alabama State College, she had long been a worker with the National Association for the Advancement of Colored People (NAACP).

Parks's refusal to give up her seat led to the intervention of the Reverend Martin Luther King Jr. and the start

THOUGH MANY AFRICAN AMERICANS NOW HOLD POLITICAL OFFICE, JUST FORTY YEARS AGO, MINORITIES WERE ROUTINELY DENIED ACCESS TO THE BALLOT BOX. AT THE DEMOCRATIC NATIONAL CONVENTION IN 1964, CIVIL RIGHTS LEADER THE REV. DR. MARTIN LUTHER KING JR. SPOKE TO PROTESTORS CARRYING PORTRAITS OF ANDREW GOODMAN, JAMES CHENEY, AND MICHAEL SCHWERNER, THREE CIVIL RIGHTS ADVOCATES SLAIN EARLIER THAT YEAR IN MISSISSIPPI.

of the civil rights movement. Eventually the movement gained momentum all over the country. Boycotts and demonstrations against discrimination sprang up everywhere. But civil rights protestors risked murder and brutality. As reported in *The Right to Vote*, "freedom riders were beaten and their buses burned; police arrested protestors by the thousands; bombs were tossed into black churches; and activists were occasionally—as in Mississippi in 1964—murdered in cold blood. . . . Discriminatory laws, arbitrary registration rulings, and threats of 'physical violence or economic reprisal' still kept most Negro citizens . . . from exercising the right to vote."

Issues such as civil rights that excite the public must be

addressed by all office seekers and especially those who run for president. From the time of the Civil War, candidates have been careful about stating their position on hot issues. How the public feels about civil rights, for instance, affects the way in which candidates campaign for the people's vote. Some try to ignore the subject, which is almost impossible with the news coverage today. Abraham Lincoln, who stood firmly against slavery, did not personally believe that blacks and whites should marry or even that African Americans should be qualified for political office.

Candidates use important issues to gain votes. Lyndon Johnson and Bill Clinton, for instance, went after the votes of African Americans in their successful campaigns. Others, such as former Alabama governor George Wallace in his unsuccessful bid for the presidency in 1968, were actively anti-civil rights to cultivate the white Southern vote. Sometimes one issue prompts a person to run for office. African-American minister Al Sharpton has had a long and mostly controversial career that has focused mainly on civil rights. In 1991 he founded the National Action Network, a civil rights organization. Since then he has run for mayor of New York City and for the U.S. Senate. Although he has been unsuccessful, he has enhanced his reputation as a prominent African-American leader.

In his civil rights speech of June 11, 1963, John F. Kennedy promised to pass a bill that would give equal rights to all. But in his campaign speeches and during the first two years of his administration, Kennedy was not an out-and-out champion of civil rights. He carefully considered the issue. He felt that the more he openly sided with the civil rights campaign, the less he would be able to work with racist Southern Democrats. After Kennedy's assassination Lyndon Johnson, a Southerner himself and the former Senate majority leader, became the man who got landmark civil rights legislation through Congress.

Because Johnson did not have to campaign (he assumed office) and because he was then elected in a landslide in 1964, it was easier for him to push the civil rights issue.

Johnson urged Congress to pass the civil rights bill. It went to the Senate in March 1964 to face the longest filibuster—83 days—in Senate history. (To delay action on a bill, congressional members may engage in endless talk on a subject, known as a filibuster.) Southern senators hoped that the rest of the Senate would not vote to cut off the filibuster (they rarely did), and that the bill would just die.

On June 21 three civil rights workers—Michael Schwerner, Andrew Goodman, and James Chaney—disappeared in Mississippi. They had been helping to register African-American voters. Their bodies were discovered by the FBI. The deputy sheriff of Neshoba County and sixteen other members of the Ku Klux Klan were indicted; seven were convicted. In the meantime, on July 2, Johnson signed the Civil Rights Act of 1964 into law. This landmark legislation outlawed discrimination based on race, color, religion, sex, or national origin.

In 1965 Congress passed a natural follow-up law, the Voting Rights Act. The violence that had followed passage of the Civil Rights Act prompted Johnson to seek further legislation. In what is considered one of his finest speeches he told Congress, "There is no Constitutional issue here. . . . There is no moral issue. . . . It is wrong—deadly wrong—to deny any of your fellow Americans the right to vote in this country."

Congress was not entirely committed to the passage of this act. But the members realized that the president was not going to back down. Not wanting the failure of the act to be viewed as the fault of Congress alone, Congress passed the bill by a vote of 77 to 19 in the Senate and 333 to 85 in the House.

The act outlaws poll taxes and literacy tests as a re-

When Catchy Words Mean Votes

Sometimes the way to win an election is just to find the right line. Come up with a catchy campaign slogan that stays in the voters' minds and doesn't let go—at least not until after election day. These are some of the most memorable—if not always successful—battle cries.

1864 Republican Abraham Lincoln said, "Don't swap horses in the middle of the stream." It meant don't desert the Union. The people didn't, but only by a narrow margin.

1884 "Ma, Ma, where's my Pa?" shouted supporters of James Blaine against Democrat Grover Cleveland. It reminded voters that Cleveland had fathered an illegitimate child. But when Cleveland won, his backers shouted, "Gone to the White House, Ha, Ha, Ha!"

1920 "Back to Normalcy" was the slogan for Republican Warren G. Harding, referring to a return to normal times after World War I.

1924 Republican Calvin Coolidge was successful with the slogan "Keep Cool with Coolidge."

1928 "A chicken in every pot and a car in every garage" promised Republican Herbert Hoover, and he won.

1936 "Sunflowers Die in November" declared the campaign of Democrat Franklin D. Roosevelt. It referred to the state flower of Kansas, home of defeated opponent Alf Landon.

1952 Supporters shouted "I Like Ike" for Republican Dwight D. Eisenhower, who beat Adlai Stevenson in the race for the White House.

1964 Barry Goldwater ran unsuccessfully against Democrat Lyndon Johnson with the slogan "In Your Heart, You Know He's Right." Johnson supporters countered with "In Your Guts, You Know He's Nuts." Johnson's own slogan that year was "All the Way with LBJ."

1976 Former peanut farmer and Democrat Jimmy Carter ousted Gerald Ford with the slogan "Not Just Peanuts."

1980 Republican Ronald Reagan campaigned against Carter with the slogan "Are you better off than you were four years ago?" The American people said no and elected Reagan.

2000 Third-party candidate Ralph Nader didn't make it with the not-so-catchy slogan "Government of, by, and for the people . . . not the monied interests."

quirement to vote. By 1968 even the most die-hard of the segregationist states, Mississippi, had registered 59 percent of its black voters. Other civil rights legislation was passed to close the discrimination gap more tightly. As noted on the History Learning Web site: "Signs such as 'Negroes need not apply' were no longer tolerated in a society becoming more and more traumatized by the Vietnam War."

The Changing Candidate Profile

Times change. Voters may become more sophisticated and knowledgeable. Issues change. What concerned voters in 1908 is probably not on the voters' minds today. But what *is* on the voters' minds today very much concerns not only the candidate but his or her party in general. Party leaders study polls and election results to determine the best way to garner more votes in the future. For instance, for many years, the Democratic Party has generally written off courting the religious-political landscape. The conservative religious votes belong to the Republicans, according to accepted belief. But that belief changed somewhat in the 2008 presidential campaign. As reported by *Time* magazine: "It has become a Democratic article of faith that it was sheer strategic stupidity to cede the values of debate to Republicans for so long. . . . The possibility that there is common ground to be colonized by those willing to look for it offers a tantalizing prospect of alliances to come . . . ." The article concludes that the decision was made to go after religious conservative voters for the 2008 election.

As time, voters, and prejudices change in America, so do candidates. The presidential campaign of 2008 presented a rare choice of candidates to the American public. Hillary Clinton, a white female senator from New York, and Barack Obama, a black male senator from Illinois, vied for the Democratic nomination. Not so long ago neither a black man nor a white woman would even have thought of running. And if they had thought of it, probably no one would have backed them. How did this slow change come about?

Old prejudices die hard. Especially in some areas of the country, prejudice remains against both blacks and women. But the American public in general no longer regards either a black person or a female as so much of an oddity that they cannot be considered for political office. And because of that change in public perception, more blacks and females than ever before are taking a run at elective offices.

Women were voting in New Zealand in 1893, long before women voted in the United States. But the New Zealand vote came about only after two decades of campaigning by women activists and organizations. The same hard work of campaigning for the vote was done in countries all over the world, such as Finland in 1906 and Canada in 1917. Indira Gandhi served three consecutive terms as India's prime minister, from 1966 to 1977, and she began to serve a fourth term, beginning in 1980, until she was assassinated in 1984.

Women's suffrage, meaning the right to vote, was finally granted in America in 1920 by the ratification of the Nineteenth Amendment. It said that the right to vote could not be denied on account of sex. As in other countries there was a long and complicated history behind that fight to get to the polls and elect a president of the United States.

A few women, such as Elizabeth Cady Stanton and Lucretia Mott, had agitated in the nineteenth century for women's right to vote. The National Woman's Suffrage Association was formed in 1869 expressly for the purpose of getting the vote. It became the National American Woman Suffrage Association in 1890. In 1913 Illinois

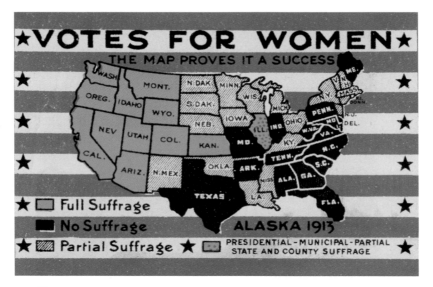

★VOTES FOR WOMEN★
THE MAP PROVES IT A SUCCESS

☐ Full Suffrage
■ No Suffrage
▨ Partial Suffrage

ALASKA 1913

☐ PRESIDENTIAL-MUNICIPAL-PARTIAL STATE AND COUNTY SUFFRAGE

THOUGH WOMEN HAVE NOW BEEN ELECTED TO RUN MANY NATIONS WORLDWIDE, THEY HAVE BEEN LEGALLY ABLE TO VOTE IN THE UNITED STATES FOR FEWER THAN ONE HUNDRED YEARS. THIS 1913 MAP SHOWS EACH STATE'S POSITION ON WOMEN'S SUFFRAGE.

became the first state east of the Mississippi to grant women the right to vote.

It was a long and often nasty fight on the way to voting rights for women in America. It took a brave woman to stand up before a hostile audience screaming that she should go back home where she belonged. And many of the outright votes against women's suffrage came from women themselves. Some just did not want to change the status quo. That was true of many men who were against suffrage; they did not want to give up control by sharing what was theirs alone. Some men regarded women as inferior. And some, men and women both, held what might today be considered amusing, if ridiculous, ideas. One such idea noted in "Arguments against Women's Suffrage"

Women Need Not Apply

If you are a woman and want to vote, it is best not to live in:

Bhutan: The rule is one vote per household, which usually means that the male votes.

Lebanon: To vote, a woman must have an elementary education. Men don't need one.

Saudi Arabia: There is no vote for women. However, in most other Muslim countries, women do have the right to vote.

HOUSE REPUBLICAN LEADER JOHN BOEHNER OF OHIO HANDS OVER THE HOUSE GAVEL TO NANCY PELOSI, DEMOCRAT OF CALIFORNIA, WHO BECAME THE FIRST FEMALE SPEAKER OF THE HOUSE ON JANUARY 4, 2007.

claimed, "If women become involved in politics, they would stop marrying, having children and the human race would die out."

Decades ago candidates, especially for higher office, did not have to consider the votes of blacks and women. That is no longer true. But it *is* true that more and more blacks and women are gaining public office—even if the push ahead can be painfully slow.

Between 1872 and 2007, a total of twenty-five women have been candidates for president of the United States. All of them ran on third-party tickets. The biggest vote-getter was Leonora Fulani of the New Alliance Party in 1988; she got 217,219 votes. Seventy-four women have run for the vice president's spot. Again, all were for third parties, with the exception of Geraldine Ferraro, who ran on the losing Democratic slate with Walter Mondale in 1984. As of 2007, there were sixteen female senators in the 100-person body, and sixty-eight women out of 435 members of the House. Nancy Pelosi became the first female Speaker of the House in 2007. Democratic Senator Hillary Clinton entered the campaign for the presidency. Also in that year the House had forty-three black members, and the Senate—and presidential campaign—had Barack Obama.

If the U.S. Congress changes significantly over the years to include more women and minority groups, the presidential campaign process will change, too. The needs and desires of those people will have to be met—or at least promised—if the candidate is ever going to take the next step.

7

Does Your
Vote Count?

Among modern democracies the United States is notorious for low voter turnout rates. For instance, in the elections of 2000 and 2004, only about 50 percent of eligible voters actually voted. Compare that with most western democracies in Europe, which have voter participation rates of over 70 percent.

Low voter turnout means that thousands of Americans who could have voted—and perhaps affected the outcome—didn't. Why don't we all exercise this most fundamental right of a democracy?

Why Don't We Vote?

In *Voice and Equality*, political scientist Sidney Verba and his coauthors list two broad areas that influence voter participation: motivation and capacity. Motivation includes how people feel about the major parties. Do they think a new party in power will make a difference for them? Do they believe that the government is listening? George W. Bush's popularity during his second term took a drastic drop. According to a Reuter's poll, his approval rating hit 24 percent in October 2007, the lowest recorded rating for any president. A Gallup poll at that time marked his rating as in the low thirties. Americans had many problems with his administration, such as the way it handled the aftermath of Hurricane Katrina in 2005. But their biggest opposition was against Bush's handling of the war in Iraq.

Capacity deals with how voters overcome the obstacles to voting, such as where polling stations are located or how easy it is for them to navigate the political system. Registration laws can be a major cause of low voter turnout. The author of *The Right to Vote* claims, "Registration laws . . . emerged in the nineteenth century as a means of keeping track of voters and preventing fraud; they also served—and often were intended to serve—as a means of keeping African-American, working-class, immigrant, and poor voters from the polls. . . . In some states, procedures were simplified and made easier; elsewhere they remained complex and difficult to navigate. . . . the laws specified when and where people could register, how often they had to register, whether or not the names of nonvoters were periodically 'purged,' the procedures to be followed if a voter moved from one precinct to another, the hours that registry offices were open, and the documentation that had to be presented to registrars."

After every election there are charges of voter fraud or flawed registration practices. In any election one party may post so-called poll watchers at various voting stations throughout the country. If a congressional race, for instance, is thought to be close in one area, poll watchers are set to challenge the credentials of likely voters. Republican poll watchers might challenge credentials in minority neighborhoods where the voters would be expected to vote

Voter Turnout in Presidential Election 2004

Citizens age 18 and over	64%
Non-Hispanic whites	67%
Blacks	60%
Hispanics	47%
Asians	44%
Age 65 and older registration rate	79%
Age 18–24 registration rate	58%
Women	65%
Men	62%
Bachelor's degree or higher	80%
High school diploma	56%
Veterans	73%

for the Democrats. These tactics are illegal; poll watchers do not have the right to demand to see a voter's ID or other proof of citizenship. But when they do make such demands or when they take photographs of those about to vote (another form of registration fraud), potential voters may be scared away.

Voter intimidation has been around for a long time; Democrats in the South used physical threats and Jim Crow laws to keep away black voters for one hundred years. And they worked. Jim Crow laws, in force between 1876 and 1965, were state and local ordinances that enforced a so-called separate but equal policy.

After the 2004 election, in which John Kerry lost to

Jim Crow laws were among the many tactics used to keep African Americans from voting in the South, and to maintain racial inequality.

the incumbent Bush, many concerns were voiced about irregularities in the voting process. Sometimes poor planning or not enough voting machines meant extremely long lines at the voting booths, discouraging some voters from participating. In some states, waiting lines in predominantly black districts were reported to be far longer than in white districts. Districts in many states cited machine malfunction so that the results were not recorded at all. There were problems with absentee ballots, which were not counted or counted too late to be part of the final tally.

Over the years many states recognized problems that keep voter turnout low. In 1977 President Jimmy Carter sent the National Uniform Registration Act to Congress. It met with disaster; most Republicans and some conservative Democrats said it would lead to corruption. A number of bills met the same end through the years. Finally, in 1993, Bill Clinton signed the National Voter Registration Act, known as the Motor Voter bill.

Motor Voter shifts the responsibility for keeping eligible voter lists from parties and campaigns to the states. It is designed to make it easier for people to get to the voting booths. Mail-in registration was extended to all states. However, North Dakota does not have registration, and Wyoming does not permit mail-in voter registration. A driver's license is proof of residence, and citizens can register at motor vehicle agencies. Voter lists are regularly updated, although this is a difficult procedure because citizens move, change names, die, or are otherwise erased from the list, as in the case of felons.

Motor Voter is not the answer to all voter participation deterrents. Even with the law, voter participation has remained fairly stable in presidential elections: 49.08 percent in 1996, 51.32 percent in 2000, and 56.69 percent in 2004. It may be that motivation is a larger factor for voters than capacity.

The Red and the Blue

The 2000 presidential election race between George W. Bush and Al Gore established a new kind of national divide, known as the red and the blue. In that bitterly contested election the country was split into so-called red states that voted Republican and blue states that voted for the Democrats. The *New York Times* published its first color presidential election map for that election. (The graphics editor said the colors were chosen because *Republican* and *red* start with the same letter.) Actually there has never been an official association between a political party and a specific color. Since September 11, 2001, however, all presidential and other candidates on campaign tours wrap themselves in the red, white, and blue—red tie, white shirt, and blue suit being a favorite—to point out their loyalty to their country.

There have always been divisions in American politics. Today, however, many states tilt strongly to one party or another, such as New York for the Democrats and Texas for the Republicans. The Solid South used to be Democratic territory. But factors such as the push for civil rights laws by Democratic presidents John Kennedy and Lyndon Johnson began the shift toward the Republicans. In 1980 about 54 percent of the South voted Republican and elected Ronald Reagan. The South has, so far, remained a Republican stronghold. The northeast has tended to shift from the GOP and vote Democratic in the last few elections.

What do these changes mean for future elections? There is no sure way to tell, although the election watchers love to predict. Alabama governor George Wallace used to say that there wasn't "a dime's worth difference between the two parties." Political scientist Philip Klinkner says today "[y]ou can always point to some rule or dynamic

RONALD REAGAN WAS THE FIRST—AND SO FAR REMAINS THE ONLY—FORMER MOVIE STAR ELECTED TO THE WHITE HOUSE. IN THIS **1982** PHOTOGRAPH, PRESIDENT REAGAN DEMONSTRATES THE GRIP HE HAD ON A FOOTBALL WHEN HE PLAYED THE GIPPER IN THE **1940** FILM *KNUTE ROCKNE ALL AMERICAN.*

in American politics that people think is enduring, until it's not."

Safe and Swing States

A safe state is one that is considered to be a reasonably sure win for either the Democratic or Republican candidate. A swing state means that no candidate has overwhelming support. In a national campaign the Republican or Democratic candidate might tend to ignore safe states, assuming that he or she will win them with little or no ac-

Key Swing States

Arkansas, in the heart of the Bible Belt and very conservative, was long a stronghold for the Democrats. Favorite son Bill Clinton, a Democrat, easily won the state in both elections in the 1990s, but George W. Bush got the state's votes in 2000 and 2004.

New Hampshire, once a reliable Republican stronghold, has been a swing state since the 1990s.

Ohio, like Missouri, is adept at choosing the next president. The state has voted for the White House winner in every presidential election since 1892, with the exception of 1944 and 1960.

Democrats have narrowly won the past few elections in Wisconsin, even though the Republican Party was founded there in 1854.

tual campaigning. For instance a Republican presidential candidate might expect to win Texas and several other Southern states even if he or she doesn't make campaign appearances there. The same candidate might well ignore Illinois, Vermont, and Massachusetts because they are traditionally liberal. He or she will probably not win no matter how much campaigning is done there. So time, money, and effort are concentrated on the swing states that could be won by either candidate. Swing states are often the key to the election. Missouri is the most reliable swing state. It has voted for the winner of every presidential election since 1904, except when it supported loser Adlai Stevenson in 1956.

Sometimes presidential and other candidates do not follow the tried-and-true campaign strategies. Sometimes a candidate will campaign vigorously in what are considered safe states because winning most of them will ensure getting enough electoral votes to win. In the general election, presidential campaigns generally focus on battleground states. But in his bids for the Republican nominations in 2004 and 2008, John McCain of Arizona chose to court the opposition. For the 2008 campaign McCain relied on the Republican tendency to nominate those who had been runner-up to the president, such as George H. W. Bush in 1988 and Bob Dole in 1996. He also courted moderates to help him win states such as New Hampshire, but still leaned toward conservatives in southern states. To get the religious right vote, he said he favored reversal of *Roe* v. *Wade*, the Supreme Court case that made abortion legal.

Voting Machines and Voting Rights

The whole voting process started with making a mark on a piece of paper. Rome used paper ballots for voting in

Check the *Ballota*!

The word *ballot* comes from the Italian *ballota*, which means "little colored ball." In Roman times a voter dropped a small clay ball into the ballot box—actually a clay pot—of his candidate. The word *blackball* also comes from this custom. To vote for a candidate in a secret society, you drop a white ball. A vote against the candidate means a black ball. We still use that term to mean excluding someone.

139 BCE. It didn't really catch on, however, until the mid–1800s, when Australia used a paper ballot. The ballot had all the candidates' names and a space to mark the voter's choice. In the late 1880s Massachusetts and New York were the first states to use the Australian-style ballot for voting.

The Myers Automatic Booth made its entrance in an election in Lockport, New York, in 1892. The voter steps into the booth and pulls a lever, which closes a curtain. Then the voter pulls the lever or levers next to the candidates' names or issues that he or she favors. Each vote is mechanically recorded. Then the voter pulls the curtain lever, the levers return to their original positions, and the curtain opens. By the 1960s more than half of the country was using lever voting machines. A number have since been replaced by computerized voting machines.

About 40 percent of voting precincts have used the punch card system. That is what caused much of the problem in the 2000 presidential election in Florida. A card with several small holes is attached to a board. Voters use a pen-shaped tool to punch out a hole or holes for their candidates. The punched-out part is called a chad. If the voter does not push heavily enough, the chad remains attached to the card—a hanging chad. Problems developed over whether or not to count hanging chads as votes. Other problems cropped up because voters mistakenly voted for two candidates on the punch card. Massachusetts, New Hampshire, and Vermont now ban the use of punch cards for voting. Other states passed laws governing manual recounts.

The 2006 midterm elections were rife with electronic voting machine problems. There were so many malfunctions in New Jersey that voters had to be turned away from the polls in some places. Houston, Texas, reported that there was no voting in one precinct because none of

FEW PEOPLE KNEW WHAT A CHAD WAS BEFORE THE 2000 PRESIDENTIAL ELECTION; NOW, CHADS HAVE BECOME PART OF U.S. HISTORY. HERE, JUDGE ROBERT ROSENBERG OF BROWARD COUNTY IN FLORIDA USES A MAGNIFYING GLASS TO EXAMINE A DIMPLED CHAD DURING THE PRESIDENTIAL VOTE RECOUNT.

the machines were operating. There were similar complaints across the country. Officials are calling for a backup paper trail for every electronic machine, with the old-fashioned paper ballot on hand in case the whole system crashes. Computer scientists are looking for new ways to make the electronic voting systems reliable and secret, and to make sure that every vote is actually counted. Dictator Joseph Stalin of the Soviet Union once remarked about elections, "It's not the people who vote that count; it's the people who count the votes."

Hanging Chads and Other Problems: The Election of 2000

It has been called by many names—none of them complimentary. It is the presidential election of 2000 between Republican George W. Bush and Democrat Al Gore. It ended with victory for Bush, who won the electoral vote but lost the popular vote. His electoral count was just one more than needed. It was one of the closest and most controversial presidential U.S. elections ever.

Americans woke up on the morning of November 8, 2000, the day after the election, without a new president. They would not have one for another five weeks. Legal and political battles at the highest levels fiercely divided the nation. The basic problem concerned counting the vote. And trouble started even before the election. A legislative aide in Mississippi discovered that more than 30,000 ballots from the last election had been discarded. Voters had mistakenly voted for two candidates on the punch card. That was a sign of what was to follow. As a *U.S. News & World Report* article commented, "No matter what the history books ultimately make of the mess in Florida, the election has already provided an instructive tutorial on the little understood but manifold flaws in the nation's voting system."

The 2000 Election
Vote Count

Popular vote:

Bush, 50,432,517 (47.81%)
Gore, 50,902,900 (48.26%)

Electoral vote:

Bush, 271
Gore, 267

Percent of eligible voters: 51.20

A vote count done soon after the polls closed gave 246 electoral votes to Bush and 255 to Gore. Florida, New Mexico, and Oregon were still too close to call. New Mexico and Oregon soon went to Gore, and it seemed that Florida's twenty-five votes would be key in deciding the election. The early tally gave the state to Bush, but by less than one-tenth of one percent. That triggered a mandatory recount. Democrats and Republicans began to squabble over how to count the chads, the small cardboard pieces punched out of punch cards. Poll workers began to study more than one million ballots in three counties—Broward, Palm Beach, and Miami-Dade. The squabbling became bizarre. If the chads were only dimpled, not indented or punched out, they would not count as votes. But if the chad was hanging—that is, punched but still attached—it would be counted as a vote. Even more bizarre, 78 chads were found on the floor of a voting room and no one knew how they got there. *U.S. News & World Report* referred to them as "homeless chads."

At the end of this turmoil of counting, thousands of presidential ballots were declared void. Voters had either voted for two candidates or hadn't used enough pressure to punch out a chad. What followed was a series of recounts and, finally, lawsuits. There were charges of ballot tampering and fraud on all sides, including some 58,000 absentee ballots that mysteriously went missing in Broward County. It all ended on December 12, when the U.S. Supreme Court stopped the recounts in Florida. The state then gave its 25 electoral votes to Bush, giving him a 271 to 267 majority in the Electoral College.

After the election the *Palm Beach Post* decided that confusion over the ballots had cost Gore the election. The paper reviewed the discarded ballots and said that more than six thousand had been cast for the Democratic nominee. Republicans disagreed with the finding.

Another loser in the 2000 election was the Voter News Service (VNS). It was set up to provide results in presidential elections so that radio and TV networks would not have to rely on polling voters as they left the booths. It was also supposed to deliver the results faster than ever before. That was possibly the downfall of VNS. Twelve minutes before the polls closed in the western part of Florida, VNS gave the state to Gore. But as the evening wore on, VNS realized its decision had been hasty and switched to Bush as the victor. When the vote got even closer, VNS changed again and decided it was just too close to call.

Its reputation already tarnished, VNS tried to count the vote via computer in the 2002 congressional election. That did not work either, and the service was disbanded.

The fiasco of the 2000 election has not yet produced any profound changes in the way candidates structure their campaigns. But it has made an inroad in better vote counting. In October 2002 Congress passed the Help America Vote Act (HAVA). It created a simpler voter registration form. It also made it easier for voters to check their registration if their names do not appear on the registration rolls. But the law has critics. Some say it replaces the troublesome punch cards with expensive electronic equipment, which can also be troublesome. They point out that electronic machines have no record of individual votes. That is because HAVA statutes do not call for a paper trail, but critics say they should.

8
Getting Out the Vote Worldwide

In a democracy the people elect their leaders directly or indirectly through representatives. According to the *Economist*, there are 122 electoral democracies throughout the world, or 64 percent of the world's states. Of them all the United States is unique in many ways. The presidential nominating process is longer here than anywhere else and is certainly more expensive. In other countries, political parties generally have tighter control over the whole election process. One nationwide vote usually elects the top leader rather than the long process of state primaries used in the United States.

In other countries that elect a president, such as France and Mexico, elections are held regularly as they are in the United States: every five years in France, every six years in Mexico. In a parliamentary democracy the leader is the prime minister or premier. He or she needs the parliament (the Congress) for direct or indirect support, which is usually expressed through a vote of confidence. The prime minister is almost always the leader of the majority party

IN THE UNITED KINGDOM, THOUGH THE PRIME MINISTER IS NOW THE PRACTICAL HEAD OF THE GOVERNMENT, TRACES OF ROYALTY REMAIN— QUEEN ELIZABETH IS THE TITULAR HEAD OF THE COUNTRY. MEMBERS OF THE HOUSE OF LORDS STILL WEAR TRADITIONAL WIGS AND ARE APPOINTED, NOT ELECTED, TO THEIR POSITIONS.

in the lower house of parliament. In a parliamentary government a distinction is generally made between the head of government and the head of state. In the United Kingdom, for instance, the head of government is the prime minister—since 2007, Gordon Brown. The head of state is the monarch, Queen Elizabeth II, coronated in 1953. Her role is largely ceremonial, and she personally exercises little political power.

Canada, Germany, the United Kingdom, and Israel are countries with a parliamentary form of government. They hold elections usually on four- or five-year schedules. However, elections are also held whenever they are needed. If the ruling party loses the confidence of the people, for instance, an election is called.

Countries with a parliamentary form of government are unicameral or bicameral. In a unicameral system parliament consists of just one house, such as the Hellenic Parliament in Greece and the Storting in Norway. Bicameral systems have a parliament with two houses. Examples are the Senate and House of Representatives in Australia, the Senate of the Republic and Chamber of Deputies in Italy, and the National Council of Provinces and National Assembly in South Africa.

Voting in Canada

Canada gained its independence from Great Britain in a process that started in 1867 and ended in 1982. It remains part of the British Commonwealth. The country is known as a parliamentary democracy and federal constitutional monarchy. This means that Great Britain's Elizabeth II is Canada's head of state, but Canada's constitution governs the country. The prime minister, who is the leader of the party in power, is the head of government.

Canada's two-house system has an appointed Senate

and an elected House of Commons. The prime minister chooses the Senate members. They are formally appointed by the governor general, who is the queen's representative in Canada. The House members are elected by a simple majority vote in an electoral district. The governor general calls for elections on the advice of the prime minister. There are no set election times, but a new election must be called within five years of the last. The dominant political parties in Canada are the Conservatives and Liberals, but the New Democratic Party (NDP) and the Bloc Quebecois are also well-represented.

Other differences between Canadian and U.S. elections include the fact that elections in Canada may be called at any time. They are generally brief (but cannot be shorter than 36 days) because the law cuts off spending for a long campaign. Canadians do not directly elect the prime minister. Instead they vote for Members of Parliament (MP), who elect the leader.

The French Way

In contrast to the British government, which goes back centuries, France is ruled by a system that dates only from 1958. That was when the Fifth Republic was formed by war hero and leader Charles de Gaulle. According to political writer Rhodes Cook, "It reflects the persona of its founder, the imperious leader of the French resistance during World War II . . . and was a reaction of sorts to the instability in the French system in the century before, when parliamentary governments rose and fell at frequent intervals." Like the first leaders of the United States, de Gaulle did not think much of political parties.

France is known as a semipresidential government system. It is divided, like the United States, into executive, legislative, and judicial branches. The executive branch is unusual, however, in that it has two leaders. The president has some direct powers, but the prime minister has the most power. The president chooses the prime minister, who is almost always from the majority party in the lower house—the National Assembly—of parliament. The upper house is the Senate.

In the original 1958 constitution the president was elected by an appointed electoral college. Since 1962 the office goes to the winner of a direct election. A president is chosen every five years. Since the direct elections began, the power and prestige of the president's office have risen. Because of winning the direct vote, the president presumably has the confidence of French citizens. This gives the office at least some control over the prime minister. All this works well if the party in power is the president's own party. Otherwise the president must choose a prime minister from the opposite party, which may result in strained power sharing.

There are a few other differences between French and U.S. national elections. In France elections are always held on a Sunday, and voters generally use paper and manual counting. Electronic voting is not widespread.

Governing Germany

Much like the United States, Germany's political system is dominated by two major parties—the Christian Democratic Union and the Social Democratic Party. This system was created in 1949 when the victorious Allied powers, which included the United States, divided the country into East and West Germany. The system was amended slightly in the 1990s when East and West Germany unified. The country is called a federal parliamentary representative democratic republic. The government is similar to that of the United Kingdom. The federal chancellor is the head of the government. Legislative power rests with the two chambers of parliament: the Bundestag (lower house) and the Bundesrat (upper house).

The chancellor heads the dominant party in the popularly elected Bundestag. German citizens do not vote for the chancellor. Instead they vote for parties and their candidates. The chosen chancellor is rarely the Bundestag leader, but is usually the head of a German state or the mayor of a large city. The chancellor is elected every five years on May 23 by the Federal Assembly. That special body contains Bundestag members plus an equal number of state delegates chosen just for the election.

The Government of Israel

The state of Israel is sometimes called a small settlement of democracy in the Middle East. Political power, as in much of western Europe, lies with the prime minister. The Knesset is the single body of parliament. In the years between 1996 and 2001 Israel elected its prime minister by a direct nationwide vote. However, direct elections were abandoned after 2001 when Ariel Sharon defeated Ehud Barak in a landslide. It was felt that direct elections did not produce a more stable government and further fragmented the Knesset.

Israel has a multiparty system. No one party has ever won enough seats (61 out of 120 members) to form a government. The party that wins the most seats must generally unite with another party or parties in order to govern. As of 2006 twelve political parties were represented in the Knesset. Israeli citizens vote for Knesset members. The party winning the most seats (generally a coalition of parties) is the party in power, and its leader becomes prime minister. Political power rests with the prime minister. Israel also has a president, but the office is largely ceremonial. The president does select the prime minister, but his or her choice is limited to the person who has the most seats won through a coalition of parliament members.

The 120 members of the Knesset are elected to four-year terms.

However, the Knesset can call for new elections before that period ends, which is not an unusual occurrence. Elections are usually called because the government in power cannot get Knesset support for a policy. If the annual budget does not get Knesset approval, that automatically means an early election.

In September 2001 the Knesset speaker, Avraham Burg, led Binyamin Ben-Eliezer of the Labor Party by about one thousand votes. But Ben-Eliezer charged that there were voting irregularities, and the count was thrown out. Officials decided to hold another primary, and Ben-Eliezer won that time. Now everyone, except perhaps Ben-Eliezer, was dissatisfied. According to political historian Rhodes Cook, "Possibly the unkindest cut of all—at least from an American perspective—came from Israel political pundits who compared the Labor Party imbroglio to the complex, confusing, and ultimately judicially settled U.S. presidential vote count the previous year. It was, they said, the latest example of a 'Florida syndrome.'"

Another difference between Israeli and U.S. elections is that Israel has an unusual balloting method. Voters get official envelopes before they enter the voting booth. Inside the booth is a tray of ballot papers, one for each party. The voter selects a paper, puts it in the envelope, and puts the envelope in the ballot box.

Voting in Mexico

From 1929 until the 2000 presidential election, one party governed Mexico. The Institutional Revolutionary Party

MEXICAN PRESIDENT VICENTE FOX WAS ELECTED FOR A SIX-YEAR TERM IN 2000, THE FIRST PRESIDENT OF AN OPPOSITION PARTY TO WIN SINCE 1920.

(PRI) had long controlled the presidency by a secretive method that allowed the incumbent to select a successor. But in the late 1900s there were signs that Mexican citizens were tiring of this process and secret control. The PRI sensed this. Ernesto Zedillo, who headed the country in 1999, announced publicly that he would not select the next president. Instead he proposed a nationwide primary.

That was not enough. For the first time since the Mexican Revolution of 1910 to 1917 the opposition defeated the party in power. The National Action Party (PAN) took control, with 43 percent of the vote compared with 36 percent for the RPI. It had also used a nationwide primary to select its leader, Vicente Fox. Overnight, Mexican citizens became directly involved in selecting their government.

Mexico is a federal presidential representative democratic republic. The leader is the president, head of state, head of the government, and commander of the military. The legislature is called the Congress of the Union. If the president's office becomes vacant during the first two years of a term, the Congress picks a substitute. The substitute must then call for a special presidential election.

The Congress of the Union has two chambers. The Chamber of Deputies has five hundred members elected for three-year terms. It is concerned with government budgets and spending. The Chamber of Senators has 128 members elected for six-year terms. It concentrates on foreign policy and confirms presidential appointments.

Another difference between Mexican and U.S. elections is that the president of Mexico is elected for one six-year term. If he or she dies or resigns during that period, Congress chooses the successor until the next election.

United Kingdom: The Grand Old Parliament

The parliament of the United Kingdom is sometimes referred to as the Mother of Parliaments because so many legislatures in other countries are modeled on it. Actually the line is a misquotation of John Bright, who delivered a speech to Parliament in 1865. What he actually said was, "England is the Mother of Parliaments," in support of demands for expanded voting rights in a country that had pioneered parliamentary government. The first elected parliament was summoned by the sixth earl of Leicester in

1265. By the reign of Edward III (1312–1377) the parliament was separated into two chambers. One was for the nobility, and the other was for knights and below. Both houses, along with the monarch, had to consent to any laws.

Today the United Kingdom is governed by a prime minister and two chambers of parliament. The upper chamber is the House of Lords, whose members are not elected by the people. The lower chamber is the democratically elected House of Commons. In theory the power of the government is vested in the Queen-in-Parliament. The queen is the head of state. But, in practice, the power lies with the House of Commons. The powers of House of Lords members are limited, and the monarch has little actual say in the making of the laws that govern the British people.

The supremacy of the House of Commons was made clear early in the twentieth century. The Commons passed a budget in 1909 that changed the tax system, making it less in favor of the wealthy. Not surprisingly the House of Lords rejected it. The following year the Liberal Party won two general elections. On that basis the Liberal prime minister, Herbert Henry Asquith, introduced a bill that put limits on the power of the House of Lords. The upper chamber refused to pass it. Asquith said he had a promise from the king to name enough liberal members to the House of Lords to erase the conservative majority. Faced with that threat the upper chamber passed Asquith's bill. It was called the Parliament Act of 1911, and it changed the way the country was governed.

Another difference between elections in Great Britain and the United States is that the English do not directly elect their head of government, the prime minister. Instead they vote for members of a political party. The leader of the winning party becomes prime minister.

Future Politics?

Is one system of electing a president or leader better than another? Would an American-style election campaign work in Germany or France or Mexico? Each democracy seems to have found its own way through the sometimes bewildering process. And for all their differences, democracies all over the world have many similarities in the way the people elect their leaders. Candidates in England and France, for instance, hit the campaign trail with as much fanfare as candidates do in the United States. Elections there may be shorter and less expensive, but they are just as noisy and full of charges hurled at opponents.

Democracies the world over also have similar problems of how to pay for campaigns and elections and how to keep them free of fraud and corruption. In the United States in the latter part of the twentieth century, the Supreme Court issued some rulings to ease these controversies. In 1962, in *Baker* v. *Carr*, the Court ruled that Tennessee had failed to reapportion the state legislature for sixty years despite its population growth. Charles Baker brought the suit, claiming that his vote was diluted because of the legislature's failure. The next year, in *Gray* v. *Sanders*, the Court said that Georgia's primary election system gave more weight to rural votes than urban votes. More rulings followed through the years in an effort to make voting rights more evenly distributed.

The Court has even looked into the touchy issue of voting rights for those convicted of crimes. However, convicted felons still make up the largest single group of U.S. citizens who cannot vote. There is also the question of rights for legally resident aliens, most of whom come from Asia or Latin America. This large group of adults cannot participate in American politics. Few areas have followed the example of Takoma Park, Maryland. A 1990 redis-

SEVERAL HUNDRED SUPPORTERS OF 2004 DEMOCRATIC CANDIDATE AL GORE PROTESTED THE STATE LEGISLATURE'S INTENTION TO NAME A SLATE OF ELECTORS FAVORABLE TO REPUBLICAN GEORGE W. BUSH, BUT THEY HAD NO EFFECT ON THE OUTCOME.

tricting survey found that voting wards of the same population often differed in the number of eligible voters because so many of them were alien residents. The city voted to allow the alien residents to vote.

There have been many suggestions for revamping the whole nominating process. Yet the old ways of politics and political campaigns do not change easily. That was evident in January 2007, with the presidential election still twenty-one months away. It was the earliest beginning of a campaign in U.S. political history. In its February 5, 2007, issue, *Time* magazine declared, "There's nearly a year to go before the Iowa caucuses, but it sure feels like the 2008 presidential-election season has reached full swing. There are at least 20 actual or assumed or wished-for candidates . . . most of them have begun raising money, hiring staff and lining up endorsements."

What was the rush? There were some unusual circumstances pushing the political hopefuls. For one thing the 2008 presidential race was wide open. There was no sitting president or vice president on the ballot, which usually has meant an uphill fight for the opposition. In the drive to be first, many primaries were held early in the year. That meant candidates had to make a name for themselves well before that time.

The rush to be heard and recognized as quickly as possible often means knocking out the opponent as quickly as possible. Campaign politics has never been a place for the easily insulted. But in this new age to get to the top first and fast, almost anything goes. And what goes first is usually civility. Some political experts say that trend is not about to change in modern political campaigns.

However, some experts believe that the early start to the 2008 campaign really didn't mean much. The public, they say, doesn't pay much attention to the candidates and the issues until a couple of months before election day. Others worry that the endlessly long campaign trail is bad for American democracy. A longer campaign and a faster schedule mean that candidates need more money to stay in the running. They need more professional—and high-priced—consultants. In the future, money will be ever more of a deciding factor in elections.

In the meantime, every four years U.S. citizens get ready for another presidential election. Prospective candidates will defend or rail against domestic issues such as health care, problems with illegal aliens, the ecology, or other future controversies. But will we really do something about election reform?

Before the first caucus or the first primary, candidates start on the long, uncertain, and often rocky road that is the American presidential election campaign. We don't seem to know how to do it any other way. So far, for all its problems and mishaps, it seems to work.

A Guide to U.S. Political Parties

America First Party. Founded in 2002 by archconservatives reportedly to eliminate corruption in the political system, it has been inactive since 2004.

American Independent Party. George Wallace of Alabama won five Southern states in 1968 for this right-wing, anti-integration, anti-Washington group. It still fields a few local state candidates.

American Nazi Party. This uniformed, swastika-wearing group had one presidential candidate, George Lincoln Rockwell, in 1964, and a party member ran for a GOP state house seat in Montana in 2006. The ANP believes that only white non-Jews of European descent should hold office.

American Party. This small, ultraconservative group—pro-life, pro-gun, and anti-taxes—took sixth place in the 1976 election but has largely faded from the political scene.

American Patriot Party. Founded in 2003, the group backs states' rights and a crackdown on illegal immigration.

American Reform Party. This group broke from Ross Perot's Reform Party in 1997, but has been relatively invisible since.

American Socialist Party. Arizona-based since its founding in 2004, this group denounces illegal immigration as a top concern.

Anti-Masonic Party. Formed in 1828 to oppose the secret society of Freemasons, it was the first third party in U.S. national politics. William Wirt from Vermont got seven electoral votes that year.

Christian Falangist Party of America. These conservative followers of Spanish dictator Francisco Franco named Kurt Weber-Heller a write-in presidential candidate in 2004.

Communist Party USA. Founded in 1924, this group reached its maximum vote total in 1932 when candidate William Z. Foster took fourth place in the election. CPUSA has not run any candidates directly since the late 1980s, but does sometimes sponsor candidates from other parties.

Constitution Party. Founded in 1992 as the U.S. Taxpayers Party, its name was changed in 1999. According to some polls, it ranks third among U.S. political parties in registered voters and is conservative on moral issues.

Democratic Party. One of two major parties in the United States, it traces origins to the Democratic-Republicans of Thomas Jefferson. Andrew Jackson was the first Democratic president elected, in 1828.

Democratic Socialists of America. A member of the Socialist International, it has never fielded any candidates for office.

Dixiecrats (formal name: the States' Rights Party). It was formed in 1948 to protest racial integration after President Harry Truman's endorsement of a civil rights plank for the Democrats. With Strom Thurmond of South Carolina heading the ticket, the Dixiecrats got thirty-nine electoral votes, but Truman won the election. The party was dissolved after that.

Family Values Party. Ultraconservative founder Tom Wells of Florida declared that God told him in 1994 to found the FVP and stop paying taxes until abortion rights end. The party is largely Wells himself, who writes in his candidacy in national and local elections.

Free Soil Party. It was formed in 1847–1848 mainly because of growing opposition to extending slavery into lands newly acquired from Mexico. Martin Van Buren, its presidential candidate, got almost 300,000 votes and helped give the election to Zachary Taylor and the Whigs. Free Soilers did elect one senator, Salmon P. Chase of Ohio. In 1854 the party was absorbed into the Republican Party.

Freedom Socialist Party/Radical Women. It was formed in 1966 by a group of women who broke from the Socialist Workers Party to follow the ideas of Marx, Engels, Lenin, and Trotsky.

Green Party of the United States. Active since the 1980s, it gained attention during Ralph Nader's bids for the presidency in 1996 and 2000. Most of its success has been at the local level, where it regularly fields candidates. It is concerned with environmental issues and decentralizing government.

Greens/Green Party USA. An older, smaller, and more leftist group than the Green Party, it supported Nader in 2000.

Independence Party. Launched by Minnesota Governor Jesse Ventura in 2000 after feuding with Perot's Reform Party, it is pro-choice, pro-gay, pro-medical marijuana, and pro-gun rights. It is essentially organized at the state level.

Independent American Party. A remnant from the American Independent Party, it exists mostly in several western states, mainly in Utah, and sponsors conservative candidates.

Knights Party. The Ku Klux Klan (KKK) is a white supremacist group against blacks, Jews, and Catholics. In the late 1800s, 1920s, and 1950–1960s it was active in politics by backing members of other parties. It created its own party in 2003, headed by Thomas Robb of the KKK, but has not yet fielded candidates.

Know-Nothing Party. Flourishing in the 1850s, the Know-Nothings were antiforeign and anti–Roman Catholic. It started as a secret organization against the influx of immigrants. When asked about the secret group, members would answer, "I know nothing."

Labor Party. Created in 1996 by labor unions, including the United Mine Workers and Longshoremen's Union, it is concerned with issues for working people. It endorsed its first national and state candidates in 1998.

Libertarian National Socialist Green Party. The group says it is atheist, pro-drug legalization, antiracist, peaceful, and pro-gay.

Libertarian Party. Along with the Greens, this group makes up the two largest third parties in the United States. Neither right nor left, members of the party are pro-choice, pro-gay marriage, pro-homeschooling, anti-gun control, and anti-income tax. 1988 LP member Ron Paul is a Republican congressman from Texas. Presidential nominee and LP member Michael Badnarik took fourth place in the election of 2004.

Light Party. Generally liberal, this group is centered around party founder Da Vid, M.D., who was a write-in presidential candidate in the elections from 1992 to 2004.

Multicapitalist Party. This party supports capitalism for all people equally.

Natural Law Party. Founded by followers of Maharishi

Mahesh Yogi, this group is sometimes referred to as a cult. Although it has endorsed candidates, the NLP announced its end as a national party in 2004.

New Party. A leftist group that advances social, economic, and political progress, it has endorsed candidates, in local elections.

New Union Party. A militant, democratic socialist party founded in 1980, it ran Jeff Miller for the Senate in Minnesota in 2006.

Pansexual Peace Party. A left-wing group that does not seem to take itself too seriously, it has not fielded any candidates.

Peace and Freedom Party. A left-wing group founded in the 1960s, it nominated Black Panther leader Eldridge Cleaver for president in 1968 and pediatrician Benjamin Spock in 1972. In 2004 it backed Native American activist Leonard Peltier.

Populist Party. Also known as the People's Party, it existed for a short time in the late nineteenth century. It was formed after an agrarian revolt that followed the collapse of agriculture prices in the Panic of 1873. Among other things the party wanted to eliminate national banks and shorten the workday to eight hours. James Weaver got more than one million votes in the 1892 presidential election.

Pot Party. A group founded on marijuana legalization, it has not yet run a candidate.

Progressive Party. There have been a number of so-called progressive parties over the past century. Best known are Theodore Roosevelt's Bull Moose Party, 1912; the Progressive Party of Wisconsin and the La Follette family, 1924; and the Progressive Party of Henry Wallace, 1948. Robert La Follette Sr. created the party so he could run in the election. He carried only Wisconsin, and the party vanished after that. The 1948 party was formed to run Wallace for the presidency. He won no electoral votes and was not helped by an endorsement from the Communist Party USA.

Prohibition Party. An ultraconservative, anti-drug, anti-communist group founded in 1869, it calls itself America's oldest third party.

Reform Party. Founded by Ross Perot in 1995, who ran as the group's presidential candidate in 1996, it backed Nader in 2004.

Republican Party, or GOP (Grand Old Party). This is one of the two major U.S. political parties, with the Democrats. Abraham Lincoln was the first Republican president elected, in 1860.

The Revolution. This hybrid group calls for legalizing drugs and prostitution (victimless crimes) and wants massive cuts in taxes and military spending cuts. The party's leader, with the whimsical pen name of R. U. Sirius, made a write-in bid for president in 2000.

Revolutionary Communist Party USA. This group follows the teachings of the late Chinese Communist leader Mao Zedong and strongly denounces capitalism.

Social Democrats USA. A part of the Socialist International, it has never offered any candidates for office.

Socialist Action Party. Founded by expelled members of the Socialist Workers Party, this communist group has fielded some local candidates.

Socialist Equality Party. Founded in 1966 as the Workers League to build a working-class order, its presidential nominee, Jerry White, got just 2,400 votes that year.

Socialist Labor Party. This militant democratic socialist party was founded in 1877 and fielded presidential candidates in every election between 1892 and 1976.

Socialist Party USA. Similar to the left-wing part of the Democratic Party, the group was founded by labor union leader Eugene V. Debs in 1900. It was once a strong third party. Former minister Norman Thomas was the party's presidential candidate in six successive presidential elections, beginning in 1928.

Socialist Workers Party. Formed in 1938, this group was originally part of the Communist Party USA. It has run presidential candidates every election year since 1948.

States' Rights Party. *See* Dixiecrats.

Stonewall Democrats. Founded in 1998 by Barney Frank, a gay member of the House, the name refers to the Stonewall riots by gay men against the police in New York City in 1969. The group advocates social change within the Democratic Party.

Third Party. Its aim is to build a new centrist party to unify America.

U.S. Marijuana Party. This group, founded in 2002, wants legalization of marijuana use and has fielded a few candidates on state ballots.

U.S. Pacifist Party. A group that opposes military action under all circumstances, it fielded write-in candidates in presidential elections for 1996, 2000, and 2004.

Veterans Party of America. Founded in 2003, it backs a political voice for all military personnel, although the party is not limited to veterans.

We the People Party. The politically central group was founded in 2000 by town councilman Jeffrey Peters of Jackson, New Hampshire, who ran for U.S. president that year.

Workers World Party. It was formed in 1959 and supports worker revolutions. Its presidential candidate, Monica Moorehead, ran in the elections of 1996 and 2000.

World Socialist Party of the USA. The group denounces violence, money, and all types of leadership, and calls for a classless, moneyless, and wageless society. They do not field or endorse candidates.

Notes

Chapter 1

p. 10, par. 1, James Madison, *The Federalist No. 10.* http://www.constitution.org/fed/federa10.htm, p. 1.

p. 14, par. 2, Evan Cornog and Richard Whelan, *Hats in the Ring: An Illustrated History of American Presidential Campaigns.* New York: Random House, 2000, p. 11.

p. 16, par. 1, "John Jay." http://www.answers/com/topic/john-jay-145K, p. 1.

p. 17, par. 2, E. E. Schattschneider, "Party Government." http://faculty.winthrop.edu/huffmons/PartiesSyllabusFall2006, p. 1.

p. 20, par. 1, http://www.reaganfoundation.org/reagan/speeches/first.asp, p. 1.

p. 21, par. 1, Cornog and Whelan, *Hats in the Ring*, p. 303.

Chapter 2

p. 24, par. 2, Richard P. McCormick, *The Presidential Game.* New York: Oxford, 1982, p. 12.

p. 26, par. 4–p. 27, par. 1, Ronald J. Hrebenar, Matthew J. Burbank, and Robert C. Benedict, *Political Parties, Interest Groups, and Political Campaigns.* Boulder, CO: Westview, 1999, p. 45.

Chapter 3

p. 40, par. 1, Louis W. Liebovich, *Richard Nixon, Watergate, and the Press.* Westport, CT: Praeger, 2003, p. 42.

p. 42, par. 1, Anthony Corrado, *Creative Campaigning: PACs and the Presidential Selection Process.* Boulder, CO: Westview Press, 1992.

p. 44, par. 2, Charles Lewis, *Political Mugging in America.* http://www.commondreams.org/views04/0306-04.htm, March 5, 2004, p. 1.

p. 46, pars. 1–2, http://www.teachablemoment.org/high/election4.html, p. 6.

Chapter 4

p. 57, par. 3, League of Women Voters, *Choosing the President 2004*, pp. 203–204.

p. 62, par. 1, League of Women Voters, pp. 129–130.

p. 62, par. 3, Hrebenar et al. *Political Parties, Interest Groups, and Political Campaigns*, p. 62.

Chapter 5

p. 66, par. 2, Liette Gidlow, "The Great Debate: Kennedy, Nixon, and Television." http://www.historynow.org/9/10/2007, p. 1.

p. 67, par. 1, Rhodes Cook, *The Presidential Nominating Process.* Lanham, MD: Rowman & Littlefield, 2004, p. 98.

p. 70, par. 4–p. 71, par. 1, Hugh Gregory Gallagher, *FDR's Splendid Deception.* New York: Dodd, Mead, 1985, p. xiii.

p. 72, par. 3, Laura Eve Pomerantz, "Roosevelt, a Presidential Campaign." http://www.teachspace.org/personal/research/poliostory/Roosevelt.html

Chapter 6

p. 75, par. 2, Alexander Keyssar, *The Right to Vote.* New York: Basic, 2000, p. 262.

p. 79, par. 4, "The 1965 Voting Rights Act." http://www.history/learningsite.co.uk/1965_voting_rights_act.htm, p. 1.

p. 79, par. 5, "The 1965 Voting Rights Act." http://www.history/learningsite, p. 2.

p. 82, par. 2, Nancy Gibbs and Michael Duffy, "Leveling the Praying Field," *Time*, 170:4, July 23, 2007, p. 28.

p. 84, par. 2, http://www.johndclare.net/women1-arguments
Against.htm, p. 3.

Chapter 7
p. 89, par. 2, Keyssar, *Right to Vote*, p. 312.
p. 91, par. 2, "Continental Divide," *Christian Science Monitor*,
July 14, 2004, p. 1.
p. 100, par. 3, David Whitman, "Chadology 101," *U.S. News
& World Report*, 129 (21), November 27, 2000, p. 34.
p. 102, par. 1, Whitman, p. 34.
p. 102, par. 2, Whitman, p. 34.

Chapter 8
p. 108, par. 2, Cook, *Presidential Nominating*, p. 122.
p. 110, par. 4, Cook, p. 133.
p. 112, par. 5, "John Bright Quotes." http://www.worldof
quotes.com/author/john.bright/1/index.html, p. 1.
p. 116, par. 1, Karen Tumulty, "Open Season," *Time*, February
5, 2007, p. 29.

All Web sites accessible as of December 1, 2007.

Further Information

Books

Aronson, Marc. *The Real Revolution: The Global Story of American Independence*. New York: Clarion, 2005.

Fradin, Dennis Brindell. *The Founders: The 39 Stories behind the U.S. Constitution*. New York: Walker, 2005.

Hillstrom, Kevin. *Defining Moments: Watergate*. Detroit: Omnigraphics, 2004.

Hinchey, Patricia H. *Student Rights*. Santa Barbara, CA: ABC-CLIO, 2001.

Matuz, Roger. *The Handy Presidents Answer Book*. Detroit: Invisible Ink, 2004.

McKissack, Patricia, and Arlene Zarembla. *To Establish Justice: Citizenship and the Constitution*. New York: Knopf, 2004.

Price-Graff, Claire. *Twentieth Century Women Political Leaders*. New York: Facts on File, 1998.

Web Sites

http://www.globalteen.net
Discusses world affairs and politics for teens.

http://www.livingroomcandidate.movingimage.us
A discussion of TV presidential commercials in the 1960s.

http://www.presidentsusa.net/campaigns.html
Information on, and the history of, primaries and conventions.

Bibliography

Books

Bartels, Larry M., and Lynn Vavreck. *Campaign Reform: Insights and Evidence*. Ann Arbor: University of Michigan Press, 2003.

Brader, Ted. *Campaigning for Hearts and Minds*. Chicago: University of Chicago Press, 2006.

Ceaser, James W., and Andrew E. Bush. *The Perfect Tie: The True Story of the 2000 Presidential Election*. New York: Roman & Littlefield, 2001.

Clements, Kendrick A. *Woodrow Wilson: World Statesman*. Boston: Twayne, 1987.

Cook, Rhodes. *The Presidential Nominating Process*. Lanham, MD: Rowman & Littlefield, 2004.

Cornog, Evan, and Richard Whelan. *Hats in the Ring: An Illustrated History of American Presidential Campaigns*. New York: Random House, 2000.

Corrado, Anthony. *Creative Campaigning: PACs and the Presidential Selection Process*. Boulder, CO: Westview Press, 1992.

Fallows, James. *Breaking the News: How the Media Undermine American Democracy*. New York: Pantheon, 1996.

Gallagher, Hugh Gregory. *FDR's Splendid Deception*. New York: Dodd, Mead, 1985.

Hertsgaard, Mark. *On Bended Knee: The Press and the Reagan Presidency*. New York: Farrar Strauss, 1988.

Hrebenar, Ronald J., Matthew J. Burbank, and Robert C. Benedict. *Political Parties, Interest Groups, and Political Campaigns*. Boulder, CO: Westview, 1999.

Judas, John B., and Ruy Teixeira. *The Emerging Democratic Majority*. New York: Scribner, 2002.

Kern, Montague, Patricia W. Levering, and Ralph B. Levering. *The Kennedy Crises: The Press, the Presidency, and Foreign Policy*. Chapel Hill: University of North Carolina Press, 1983.

Keyssar, Alexander. *The Right to Vote*. New York: Basic, 2000.

Lasky, Victor. *J.F.K. The Man & the Myth*. New York: Macmillan, 1963.

League of Women Voters. *Choosing the President 2004*. Guilford, CT: Lyons, 2003.

Levin, Phyllis Lee. *Edith and Woodrow: The Wilson White House*. New York: Scribner, 2001.

Liebovich, Louis W. *Richard Nixon, Watergate, and the Press*. Westport, CT: Praeger, 2003.

Mayer, Jeremy D. *Running on Race: Racial Politics in Presidential Campaigns, 1960–2000*. New York: Random House, 2002.

McCormick, Richard P. *The Presidential Game: The Origins of American Presidential Politics*. New York: Oxford University Press, 1982.

Merzer, Martin, et al. *The Miami Herald Report: Democracy Held Hostage*. New York: St. Martin's, 2001.

Olsen, Keith W. *Watergate: The Presidential Scandal that Shook America*. Lawrence: University of Kansas Press, 2003.

Pitney, John J. Jr. *The Art of Political Warfare*. Norman: University of Oklahoma Press, 2000.

Preimesberger, Jon, ed. *National Party Conventions*. Washington, DC: Congressional Quarterly, 1995.

Reichley, A. James. *The Life of the Parties: A History of American Political Parties*. New York: Free Press, 1992.

Smith, Gene. *When the Cheering Stopped: The Last Years of Woodrow Wilson*. New York: Time, 1964.

Verba, Sidney, Kay Lehman Schlozman, and Henry E. Brady. *Voice and Equality: Civic Voluntarism in American Politics*. Cambridge, MA: Harvard University Press, 1995.

Ward, Geoffrey C. *A First Class Temperament: The Emergence of Franklin Roosevelt*. New York: Harper, 1989.

Whitney, David C. *The American President*, 8th ed. Pleasantville, NY: Reader's Digest, 1993.

Wormser, Richard. *The Rise and Fall of Jim Crow*. New York: St. Martin's, 2003.

Articles

"The Accidental President." *Economist*, 357(820l), December 16, 2000.

Bateman, Herman E. "Observations on President Roosevelt's Health During World War II." *Mississippi Valley Historical Review*, 43 (1), June 1956, pp. 82–102.

Buschini, J. "The Spanish-American War." Small Planet Communications, Inc., 2000. http://www.smplanet.com/imperialism/remember.html (Accessed January 22, 2007).

Clare, John D. "Arguments against Women's Suffrage." Green-field History Site. 2002/2006. http://www.johndclare. net/Women1_ArgumentsAgainst.htm (Accessed January 12, 2007).

Democratic National Committee. "The Democratic Party: Our Party." Democratic Party Web site. 1995–2007. http:// www.dnc.org/ourparty.html (Accessed December 10, 2006).

Drudge, Matt. "Newsweek kills story on white house intern: 23-year-old, former White House intern, sex relationship with President." *Drudge Report*, January 17, 1998. http://www.drudgereportdrudgereportarchives.com/data/2 003/06/04/20030604_135223_ml.htm (Accessed December 10, 2006).

George, Juliette L. et al. "Issues in Wilson Scholarship." *Journal of American History*, 70(4), March 1984, pp. 845–853.

Gibbs, Nancy, and Michael Duffy. "Leveling the Praying Field." *Time*, 170:4, July 23, 2007.

Gidlow, Liette. "The Great Debate: Kennedy, Nixon, and Television." *History Now*. The Gilder Lehrman Institute of American History, 2004. http://www.historynow.org/09_ 2004/historian2.html (Accessed January 3, 2008).

Greenfield, Jeff. "The Fit-President Theory." *Men's Health*, 19(9), November 2004, pp. 106–110.

Howley, Kerry. "In defense of attack ads." *Reason*, 38(1), May 2006, p. 15.

Huckshorn, Robert J. "Who Gave It? Who Got It?" *Journal of Politics*, 47(3), August 1985, pp. 773–789.

"John Bright Quotes." WorldofQuotes.com. http://www.world ofquotes.com/author/John-Bright/1/index.html (Accessed January 20, 2007).

Kennedy, Robert F. Jr. "Was the 2004 Election Stolen?" *Rolling Stone*, 1002, June 15, 2007, pp. 46–51.

Lewis, Charles. "Political Mugging in America, Anatomy of an 'Independent' Smear Campaign." CommonDreams.org News Center, March 6, 2004. http://www.common dreams.org/views04/0306-04.htm (Accessed January 3, 2008).

Matthews, Donald R. et al. "Political Factors and Negro Voter Registration in the South." *American Political Science Review*, 57 (2), June 1963, pp. 355–367.

Nordhaus, R. Edward. "S.N.C.C. and the Civil Rights Movement in Mississippi." *History Teacher*, 127(1), November 1983, pp. 91–102.

Parmet, Herbert S. "The Kennedy Myth and American Politics." *History Teacher*, 24(1), November 1990, pp. 31–39.

Pomerantz, Laura Eve. "Roosevelt, A Presidential Campaign." http://www.teachspace.org/personal/research/poliostory/roosevelt.html (Accessed January 25, 2007).

Reagan, Ronald. "First Inaugural Address." Presidential inaugural address at the U.S. Capitol, Washington, D.C., January 20, 1981. Document provided by The Ronald Reagan Presidential Library and Foundation. http://www.reaganfoundation.org/reagan/speeches/first.asp (Accessed January 2007).

Republican National Committee. "The Republican Party—GOP history." Republican Party Web site. http://www.gop.com/About/AboutRead.aspx?AboutType=3 (Accessed December 10, 2006).

Rutenberg, Jim. "Internet Ad Attack: In Politics, the Web is a Parallel World with its Own Rules." *New York Times*, February 22, 2004.

Summers, John H. "What Happened to Sex Scandals? Politics and Peccadilloes, Jefferson to Kennedy." *Journal of American History*, 87(3), December 2000, pp. 825–854.

Theilmann, John et al. "Campaign Tactics and the Decision to Attack." *Journal of Politics*, 60(4), November 1998, pp. 1050–1062.

Trueman, Chris. "The 1965 Voting Rights Act." History Learning Site, 2000–2007. http://www.historylearningsite.co.uk/1965_voting_rights_act.htm (Accessed December 2006).

"2004 Presidential Election." The Center for Responsive Politics. http://www.opensecrets.org/presidential/index_2004.asp?graph=spending (Accessed December 2006).

"A ways to go/electronic voting machine problems (editorial)." *Houston Chronicle*, November 8, 2006, p. 8.

Weiss, Peter. "Ballot roulette." *Science News*, 170 (19), November 4, 2006, pp. 298–300.

Whitman, David. "Chadology 101: Divining a Dimple." *U.S. News & World Report*, 129(21), November 27, 2000, p. 34.

"Woodrow Wilson, 1913–21." Health Media Lab: Interactive

Health Education. http://www.healthmedialab.com/exhibits -p-wilson.html (Accessed January 22, 2007).

Young, Louise M. "Women's place in American politics: The Historical Perspective." *Journal of Politics*, 38(3), August 1976, pp. 295–335.

Index

Page numbers in **boldface** are illustrations, tables, and charts.

About the Author

A former U.S. Navy journalist and children's book editor, **Corinne J. Naden** lives in Tarrytown, New York. She is the author of more than ninety nonfiction books for young readers. Her most recent book for Marshall Cavendish was *Patients' Rights,* in this series.